Church Leavers

Faith journeys five years on

Alan Jamieson
Jenny McIntosh
Adrienne Thompson

First published in Great Britain in 2006

Society for Promoting Christian Knowledge
36 Causton Street
London SW1P 4ST

First published in New Zealand in 2006 by The Portland Research Trust,
Wellington, New Zealand as *Five Years On: Continuing faith journeys of those
who left the church* by Alan Jamieson, Jenny McIntosh and Adrienne Thompson

British Library Cataloguing-in-Publication Data
A catalogue record for this book is available from
the British Library.

ISBN-13: 978–0–281–05864–8
ISBN-10: 0–281–05864–4

1 3 5 7 9 10 8 6 4 2

Editing and text design: Kapiti Print Media Ltd

Printed in Great Britain by Ashford Colour Press

ALAN JAMIESON is a pastor who has trained as a sociologist and written previously about church leavers and faith crisis in *A Churchless Faith* (2002) and *Journeying in Faith* (2004).

JENNY MCINTOSH is the facilitator of Spirited Exchanges, the umbrella name of a number of initiatives for those grappling with faith and church issues. She is an advocate for people in this marginal place.

ADRIENNE THOMPSON is a spiritual director engaging with people in and out of church and on the edges. She is also a writer and editor.

All three live in New Zealand and participate in the Wellington Central Baptist Church.

We are grateful for permission to reprint Jenny Bornholdt's poem *Weighing Up The Heart*.

Many people have been involved in bringing this book to life. We want to thank each of you very much.

Five groups stand out for particular thanks. First, the people whose stories make up this book: thank you for your time, your willingness to tell your own stories and for allowing us to weave your stories into this book.

Secondly, thank you to John Sinclair who suggested we do this study and was part of the initial analysis of the responses.

We are very grateful to the Dove and Portland Trusts who have financially and practically supported this project.

To Ken Edgecombe and Chris Benge we want to say thank you for your editiorial eye, suggestions and comments. Again thank you to Alison Barr, Acquisitions Editor at SPCK, for her ongoing encouragement and support of Alan's writing.

Finally we would like to thank the communities within Spirited Exchanges and Wellington Central Baptist, with whom we journey.

Contents

Foreword

RESEARCH ON PEOPLE'S FAITH JOURNEYS is rare and what follows is the first study of its kind. While some research has been done with those who leave evangelical churches in the western world there is none, to our knowledge, that has tracked the journeys of leavers over a significant period of time.

This study seeks to fill this gap. Looking at the experience and views of church leavers provides real insights both into why some people depart and why others wouldn't consider coming in the first place. The study follows a number of church leavers over a five year period. It investigates whether these people have reconnected with church and whether they have formed or found other meaningful faith groups. It considers their current beliefs and practices and compares and contrasts their views on prayer, mission, church, human nature, leadership, the Bible, and God.

From this study, we have made tentative conclusions about the faith trajectories of people who leave evangelical churches. Some readers will no doubt compare their own experiences with the stories of faith shared here. If this is why you are choosing to read this book we hope these stories will enrich your own journey, offering both hope and insight.

Others will read with a more detached or professional eye. Whether you are involved in research, pastoral ministry, church leadership, shaping emergent forms of church, or spiritual direction we hope the mix of findings, analysis, direct quotes and our own reflections will be useful in your work.

Foreword

As a new spiritual landscape is opening up across the western world we are finding that church leavers are playing an increasing role. George Barna's most recent book *Revolution: Finding Vibrant Faith Beyond the Walls of the Sanctuary*[1] suggests a sea change is upon us in the "way people anchor their faith pursuits" (p 61). His research in the United States suggests that by 2025 seventy percent of American Christians' primary means of spiritual experience and expression will not be through a local church. If Barna and other Christian commentators anticipating a similar revolution are even remotely right then it is crucial we come to understand church leavers and their continued journeys of faith in order to prepare for the new realities of a fundamentally different spiritual landscape.

Introduction

WHAT HAPPENS TO THE CHRISTIAN FAITH of people who leave church?
A Churchless Faith began to answer that question. This book further
develops that answer.

It began with a conversation over a cup of coffee. Someone
wondered what had happened to the 108 people who participated in
Alan Jamieson's original research. Alan agreed it would be interesting to
do a follow up study and find out.

For a variety of reasons (explained in Chapter One) it wasn't possible
to do face to face interviews, so Alan decided to ask for written responses.
He and Jenny McIntosh devised questions that invited people to reflect
on their beliefs, practices and experience and compare the present with
five years earlier when they had been interviewed for the original study.[2]
Both Alan and Jenny considered the responses and together agreed
where people might best be placed in the categories of church leavers
developed for the first research. Some people still matched the position
they had fitted five years earlier. Others had moved.

Adrienne Thompson was then asked to do a detailed analysis of the
individual questionnaires.

Originally Alan had envisioned a lengthy article for an academic
publication, but as it developed we sensed it might interest a wider
audience. As well as amplifying Alan's original research it could provide
a valuable resource for pastors, spiritual directors, people involved in
church leadership, people supporting those who struggle with church
and faith and of course, and very importantly, for church leavers. It

became clear that what we had actually conceived was not an article but a book that, like *A Churchless Faith*, made the research accessible to anyone who was interested, but more than that, offered reflections on the meaning and potential of the research.

It was a long gestation. Draft after draft clogged our computers. We knew we had here something of value, but what shape would it take? Then we realised the title given to the study of the church leavers – *Five Years On* – applied with equal force to the account of our experiments in finding ways to support them. Five years on, what have we learned and what are we doing?

Thus this book not only tells the stories of people who left church but describes the beginning and the development of Spirited Exchanges, an initiative to support church leavers. This project continues to grow. Several groups now meet regularly. The newsletter has an ever-growing subscription list in New Zealand and overseas with readers in and out of the established churches. In the UK a group of people are actively working to establish a similar initiative based on the research and principles of Spirited Exchanges.

The book is divided into three parts. Part One describes the two research projects. Chapter One summarises the findings of the original study. Chapter Two introduces the follow-up study in which people were asked how their faith had changed during the five years between the research projects.

Part Two presents the research findings. Each chapter picks up and analyses an aspect of Christian faith from the perspective of those who took part in the study. The findings are illustrated by direct quotes from respondents.

Part Three moves beyond academic analysis to reflect on the implications of the research. Here Jenny recounts the story of Spirited Exchanges. The three authors each contribute a chapter from our individual perspectives as pastor, facilitator of Spirited Exchanges, and spiritual director.

Introduction

Actually the book has multiple authors. Much of the text consists of direct quotations from the spoken or written words of those who participated in the studies. These people are identified by pseudonyms. Three names appear on the cover as the authors. We have each written different sections (identified in the chapter headings) but all of us have scrutinised and discussed the text intensively, made comments and suggestions and worked together on form, content and structure. Many meetings and many, many emails and phone conversations have brought this book into being.

This book makes available what we've learned, and are still on the road to learning, over the last five years concerning the faith journeys of church leavers and how we may support them.

INTRODUCING THE RESEARCH

1 A Churchless Faith

(Alan)

"PEOPLE ARE LEAVING THE CHURCH." Ten years ago, despite the almost mantra-like quality of this statement in the media and among religious statisticians, there appeared to be little understanding about who was leaving, or when, or why, or what happened to them after they had gone. Of course everyone had a view on these issues but few, especially church leaders, had actually sat down and talked with those who went.

It's important early on to define what we mean by 'church'. To do this we need to distinguish between three terms: 'Church'; established church; and post-church groups.

From a theological perspective all followers of Christ (Christians, from the Greek *christianoi*: 'Christ people') are by definition part of the Church – the house or community of the Lord (from the Greek *Kyriake*: 'belonging to Kyrios: the Lord'). This is the Church universal – the church made up of all those who belong to Christ.

'Established church' is here defined as those churches which function in established ways. They have established organisational, leadership, legal, financial and liturgical structures which operate in a consistent way as churches have for the last century or more in western societies. Typically the organisational structures of established churches include specific buildings ('churches'); specific and often paid roles (priests, ministers or pastors); financial systems (often with charitable tax status); constitutions; and formal connections with other similarly structured and constituted churches (denominations).

Later in the book we will be encountering different kinds of post church groups. Describing a person or group as 'post-church' indicates that their previous participation in an 'established church' context has ceased. Post-church is here distinguished from 'post-Christian' or 'post-faith'.

Before I began interviewing people who had left established churches I too thought I knew what happened to the Christian faith of those who went. Although I had more than once thought about moving out myself, deep down I believed that leaving was inevitably the first step to a dwindling faith and the ultimate Christian failure: 'backsliding'.[3]

I concluded my first interview with actual church leavers somewhat bewildered. The couple I had just met didn't fit my expectations. They had left their eldership role in a growing Pentecostal church five years earlier, yet their faith had obviously continued to develop; they had an ongoing sense of God at work in their lives, and they were involved in their community as an expression of their faith.

I was intrigued and somewhat mystified; my plan to conduct a quick study with a few church leavers in order to confirm my prejudices was in disarray. In fact the study went on to become a major project involving 162 interviews with both church leavers (108 interviewees) and leaders (54 interviewees) in Evangelical, Pentecostal and Charismatic churches (a group which I refer to as EPC churches).

The people interviewed were predominantly in their 30s and 40s. They had made Christian commitments, as well as commitments to their respective churches, as adults (over the age of 18 years) and had been actively involved in their churches for an average of 15.8 years.

To sum up the faith journeys of 108 people is a complex task. Each person's experience was quite distinctive, with its own twists and turns.

However, it became evident that church leavers fell into five distinct groups. In order to make sense of all that follows these five categories of leavers are introduced below.

1. DISPLACED FOLLOWERS

In *A Churchless Faith* I named the first group of leavers 'Disillusioned Followers'. They are *followers* because the faith they continue in has not substantially changed from the faith they followed within their earlier churches. On reflection I have changed the word *disillusioned* for *displaced,* which gives a more complete picture of this group. They are called ***displaced*** because events and circumstances have convinced them to leave the EPC style of church even though they continue to hold great affinity with it.

There were 19 people in this group of leavers, or 17.5% of those interviewed. They left in two major categories:

- The ***hurt*** – those whose expectations of particular care or support from the church body in times of need were disappointed.
- The ***angry*** – those who left the church in disagreement with the leadership of their church because of the direction, vision or leadership structure of either their church or of EPC churches in general.

Both the 'hurt' and the 'angry' can be said to have left because of specific grumbles[4] with the church. These grumbles centre on the leadership, direction and operating nature of the church.

The level of critique of these people does not extend to questioning the whole basis of Evangelical, Pentecostal and Charismatic faith itself. On the contrary, such leavers use these understandings of what the church "should" be as the foundation for their claim that their particular church has failed.

The Displaced Followers continue in a received faith. They have not disengaged from the faith they practised in church. The faith they received when they made their decision to follow Christ and join the church is the same faith they follow today as church leavers. Typically, such a faith is based on an external authority beyond themselves such as the Bible, the tradition of their church, or the teaching of their pastor.

When describing their faith the Displaced Followers, by definition, gave very clear statements of a conservative evangelical Christian faith. For example, Steve said that his faith was "based on God's word and reinforced experientially as I have seen His faithfulness personally and known His love . . . . Jesus is the way, the truth and the life. His word stands. It is an absolute with no compromise."

Laura also held to a deliberate acknowledgement of Scripture: "The Bible clearly states that it alone is God's word and that Jesus Christ is God's Son as revealed in it – 'I am the way, the truth and the life – no one comes to the Father but by ME!' This sums it up for me."[5]

Gwyn said her faith was based on God's word and on outworking its teaching in personal experience. "Personal relationship with God and Jesus, the leading of the Holy Spirit and the acceptance and embracing of all scripture," were foundational to her.

Yet despite these very clear statements of an EPC type of faith, the Displaced Followers remain alienated from church.

> *Gwyn*   I believe the church has lost its way and its purpose. Too much of man and the world system. Not totally scripturally based.
>
> *Laura*   [said her view of church is the same as five years ago] It does not meet real needs of people. I personally was glad <u>not</u> to be a part of a local church during the previous year . . . . Have been to a few Sunday morning meetings in various churches but have felt frustrated by the subtle misleading of the teaching.

While not attending or belonging to a church, these people's faith remains dependent on the broader EPC community. A whole variety of such sources of dependency is available to them including major seminars, trans-church based groups such as Promise Keepers, Christian workshops, books, magazines, television and radio programmes and preachers.

While the Displaced Followers remain externally dependent on this wider EPC community they also remain internally dependent on the personal disciplines encouraged by the EPC church. These include either the continued practice of 'quiet times' or the sense of obligation to them,[6] financial giving (beyond friends and family), service to others, personal witness, and so on.

Despite this group's antipathy to the church there is a clear recognition of the need to be part of some faith group outside the established church where they can share their faith with others of similar belief.

> *Anne-Marie* Study groups are necessary for foundation of faith.

> *Steve* Growing awareness in the understanding of how God's church should be working and where some of our blind spots have been. Frustrated at my own lack of involvement but I feel I am still in a place of learning from God about His church.

> *Laura* Have been committed to Bible Study Fellowship International as a women's leader . . . my driving motivation is to help others know and have faith in the word of God (Bible) to be equipped in all of life's circumstances.

These comments indicate the concerns of the Displaced Followers. They remain thoroughly convinced and committed to a conservative evangelical Christian faith yet they have been disappointed by and remain alienated from the established church. This is despite their desire to be part of a Christian group or gathering.

The post-church faith of the Displaced Followers is an unchanged faith. Their grumbles centre on the church rather than on the assumptions of the EPC faith.

The final aspect of the faith of the Displaced Followers is boldness in their own faith. By this I mean that they are very clear and definite about their Christian faith and the correctness, from a Christian perspective, of their decision to leave the church. Of all the groups of leavers, it is members of this group who typically quoted a number of passages from

Scripture to reinforce their present faith position and the rightness of their decision to leave the church. Throughout the rest of this discussion the displaced followers will simply be called the Displaced.

2. REFLECTIVE EXILES

> *Melanie* The word Christian has various meanings depending on the person. I'm not sure what stage I'm at now. I went through a stage where I didn't feel like I was a Christian because I wasn't doing this or that. But I think I'm at a stage where I really deeply believe in the message of the scriptures. I still think in many ways I still live like a Christian. But I wouldn't have the audacity to call myself one. I'm not even sure what a Christian is anymore. I think going to church a lot of the time. Or even not going to church. A lot of our Christianity can be a like a sub-culture. I was trying to work out what is actual faith and what is Christianity. So I'm sort of wading through that at the moment. I feel like a lot of things have been stripped away and I'm not sure how much of a skeleton I've got left. I think it will take time. To be honest I think a lot of time I just get up and go to work and come home and get on with life. I'm not passionately moved like I used to be to do things for God anymore. But I don't think I'm closed or distant either. Which sounds a bit sad. But I'm not hung up like I used to be. Most of my Christian life I felt terribly inadequate and condemned.

The second category of leavers, those like Melanie, may be named 'Reflective Exiles'. This group made up 32 of the original 108 interviewees. Reflective Exiles leave their churches for quite different core reasons from the Displaced. Although they too may have problems with the leadership, direction and practice of their church or of EPC churches in general, these issues are not fundamental in their decision to leave.

For this group of leavers, and for those in the next category (Transitional Explorers), leaving is typically a process which occurs over a long period of time, perhaps 18 months or more.[7] This process of moving away from the church begins gradually with feelings of unease, a sense of disconnection between church and what happens in other important areas of their lives, and a reducing sense of fit and belonging to the church community and its 'faith package'.

I called the gateway through which this group leaves the church **Meta-grumbles**. These are not grumbles about specific issues within the church,[8] nor are they questioning peripheral aspects of EPC faith. These are questions about the deep rooted foundations of the faith itself. Such concerns go to the core of their faith.

They are called *reflective* because of the questioning of their faith which now characterises them. And they are called *exiles* because they are, albeit by personal choice, exiled from a community and a previously satisfying belief system. This includes the erosion of a way of understanding themselves, their life and their God which had been very important, even foundational, to them in the past.

The faith of the Reflective Exiles can be characterised, in contrast to the Displaced, as counter-dependent. Where the Displaced Followers remained dependent on the wider EPC community, the Reflective Exiles are pushing against anything from that quarter. When I asked this group of leavers what nurtures their faith now, the most common response was "It certainly isn't . . ." followed by some description of aspects of the wider EPC community and the personal faith disciplines which it endorses.

Secondly, the Reflective Exiles are engaged in deconstructing their previous faith. That is, they are engaged in a process of taking to pieces the faith they had received, accepted and acted within for so many years. This a very destabilising experience. Their faith has been an important part of their world view, the foundation of important life decisions and an integral part of their sense of selfhood. Now they are involved in an ongoing reflective process which involves a re-evaluation of each component of their faith.

Finally, and not surprisingly, their faith is very hesitant. Many spoke of having "put it [their faith] all down for a while and leaving it", because it got too confusing and disillusioning. Because of feelings like this, their ownership of their faith is somewhat tentative.

Throughout the remainder of this discussion the Reflective Exiles will be called Exiles.

3. TRANSITIONAL EXPLORERS

The third group of leavers was called *Transitional Explorers*. These interviewees displayed an emerging sense of ownership for their faith. They are less tentative, increasing in confidence. These people have made a clear decision to negotiate a new *transition* – moving on from deconstructing the received faith they once held and giving energy instead to *exploring* a new self-owned faith.

To varying degrees this faith incorporates elements of the previous church-based faith. The individual has now tested these elements, however, and found them valid and worthy to be retained. The internal jury has reached a verdict on these faith elements and now accepts them as plausible, beyond reasonable doubt. Of course, what constitutes reasonable doubt varies from person to person. For some, the examination process involves rigorous theological and philosophical debate through reading and interaction with others. For others, reasonable doubt is based more on personal experience and what is plausible to them at an intuitive level or through a deeper trust of their own feelings.

The transitional explorer faith stance indicates that the internal jury has begun to reach a decision on at least some of the elements of faith and is returning a verdict of personal appropriation: "This is something I can hold to".

The 19 Transitional Explorers represented 18% of those interviewed. For the remainder of the book this group will be called the Explorers.

4. TRANSITIONING TO AN ALTERNATIVE FAITH

Alongside these Transitional Explorers was a small group of those who were *transitioning to alternative faith*. This grouping in the original study[9] was made up of two people who had moved to a more 'new age'[10] outlook and five who had so many questions, doubts and issues with the Christian faith that they were best characterised as agnostic in their belief system.

5. INTEGRATED WAYFINDERS

I called the final category of leavers *Integrated Wayfinders*. Where Transitional Explorers are in the process of reconstructing their faith and developing an emerging self-ownership, Integrated Wayfinders have largely completed this process. While there is a sense in which the 'integrated faith' is also still open and being constantly redefined and adapted, they have traversed the most critical stage of the journey.

The whole process could be likened to building a house out of the timber from a previous one. The first part of the process requires moving out of the old home and carefully tearing it down. In the demolition phase the timber, window and door frames, roofing materials and fittings are assessed for their usefulness as materials for the new house – the 'reflective phase'. The next part of the process involves building the new house, out of material retrieved from the old one and by incorporating a body of new material. This is the 'transitional phase', where much of the structural faith building is done. Finally the house is complete and the person is able to move in. This final phase may include minor ongoing work to the house; rooms may still need to be painted, repairs made and at times modifications of various degrees may be necessary. Although this work is ongoing, the basic structure of the home is complete and it now affords a safe place for the individual to live.

This phase in the faith journey was called the 'integrated faith' phase, because here the structure of the faith is largely complete and the person is able to claim it and own it. People at this stage, like the builder of the home, may well experience ongoing questioning and occasional periods of faith re-evaluation (sometimes quite substantial re-evaluations), but they will not need to do the major structural work again.

The term 'integrated' also describes a second aspect of these people's faith, in that they are seeking to integrate their faith into all aspects of their lives. Theirs is a fully rounded faith. These people, like no other group previously discussed, intentionally express physical, mental, emotional, sexual, relational and spiritual aspects of their selfhood in ways that are deeply connected with their faith. Hence people at this faith phase are very aware of the deeper personal issues that lurk within themselves.

Geoff's description of the key elements of his faith is typical of the Integrated Wayfinders:

> *Geoff* – key components of my faith are:
> - being part of a regular faith community, meeting regularly and sharing something of life's struggles and joys, both spiritual and human
> - being able to rejoice in my humanity
> - having a prayer life, which does go up and down, trying to discern the voice of God to me through reading the scriptures often, spiritual reading, occasional theological reading.

The term 'wayfinder' may seem at first somewhat curious. It is intended to signal that the people in this faith position have found something of a way forward in their faith. Throughout the remainder of this discussion this group will simply be called Wayfinders.

A seamless, turbulent and dynamic process

Assigning people to these major categories of church-leavers may appear to make a very fluid and dynamic process into an ordered and sequential movement from one box to another. This is certainly not what it feels like for the people involved. For them the process is anything but a neat jump from box to box. It is, as one person described it, like being "adrift on the sea", tossed by the ocean waves, blown by the changing winds and pulled by hidden currents. Each person moves this way and that, perhaps more aware of an overall turbulence than any clear directional path. It is often only in hindsight that we can discern the path we have travelled and are able to make sense of our journey and faith in new ways.

At such turbulent points of faith a map can be enormously helpful to give a context for our personal crises. The good news is that Christians through the centuries have described their faith journeys in remarkably similar ways. Having access to these descriptions can normalise an individual's personal experience. It can alleviate the anxiety that "I'm losing my faith". People who have assumed that all their doubts and questions are simply their own fault, or result from some personal sin, evil or abnormality in their Christian life, can gain a different perspective.

The 'map' I have used to explain why people leave particular churches at particular points is drawn from Professor James Fowler's work on the stages of faith. Fowler is a Christian theologian and a psychologist who for many years worked on developing an understanding of the stages or phases of faith that many people move through in their lifetime. Together, the stages form a framework that many people find enormously helpful. Those who wish to look into this area further could go to *A Churchless Faith* for more detail.

For Fowler faith is more than a set of beliefs, it is a way of living that affects the whole of a person's life. 'Faith' therefore is not a noun but a verb, because faith involves loving, trusting, believing, acting and suffering. It includes a person's intellect, emotions and volition. When we speak of 'faith' in this book we too are using this more dynamic understanding drawn from Professor Fowler.

Having discussed the original study and the categories of leavers that it identified,[11] we can now move to the return study five years later.

DISPLACED FOLLOWERS	REFLECTIVE EXILES	TRANSITIONAL EXPLORERS	INTEGRATED WAYFINDERS
Dependent Faith	Counter-dependent Faith	Inner-Dependency	Inter-Dependency
Received Faith	Deconstruction of Faith	Reconstruction of Faith	Integrated Faith
Unexamined Faith	Self-examining	Emerging self ownership	Autonomous Faith
Bold	Hesitant	Strengthening	Strong

2 Five Years On

(Alan)

THE IDEA TO RETURN AND INTERVIEW PEOPLE five years later came from a member of a Spirited Exchanges group in Wellington. Over a coffee he suggested going back and seeing where the people in the original study were now. The ideal would have been to re-interview each person face-to-face, but limited time and money made such an exercise completely impossible. Over the intervening years many of the interviewees had moved location so that meeting them would require a large amount of travelling. Coupled with this, interview scripts would need to be transcribed[12] and then carefully analysed. In the face of these difficulties we decided to send an open-ended questionnaire to each respondent. Using this method would require no travel, no interviews and no transcribing time. It would also undoubtedly mean a lower respondent return rate than a personal invitation to be interviewed.

A fuller account of the methods used is discussed in Chapter 15. At this point only a brief summary is provided.

We sent out questionnaires to the original 108 interviewees. A number of factors affected the response rate (these are further discussed in Chapter 15). Firstly a large number of people had changed address over the five-year period and we were unable to contact them despite numerous efforts. Secondly the questionnaire was extensive, asked very personal questions and demanded a lot of thought. Despite these difficulties we received 47 completed questionnaires, representing 66%

of those for whom we had a correct address. This is a very high return rate for research of its type.

In the original research a small group of the people interviewed were on the verge of leaving (ten of the original 108) or had left for a short period of time and subsequently rejoined a church (eight of the original 108). Six people in these two categories are part of the follow-up study. All six were part of established church communities five years later.

The concerns of three of these people were primarily to do with church, church structures and church dysfunction. Specifically they were concerned about a desire for more thoughtful and content-rich teaching. They also had some minor quibbles with the ethical lines drawn by Pentecostal churches – for example, banning alcohol or forbidding unmarried couples to live together. There was no indication of major dissatisfaction with God or the Christian faith in particular core essentials.[13] Five years later their stance has remained the same – perhaps even been solidified. In this sense the best category for these people's present faith is what will be called the 'Returnees' category. This represents a return to participation in an EPC church, a no-change situation from five years ago. The following comment by Graeme reflects the faith position of these respondents:

> *Graeme* Our beliefs remain the same but having questioned much of theology then and now, we have come out from being under the law and live by grace. . . . Five years on we find prayer not so ritualistic but rather companionable. . . . God is interested in every part of our lives and it is a joy to have fellowship with him. He never leaves us nor forsakes us . . . we have seen growth in our personal holiness, and change in our attitudes of what we do and say, how we treat others (not judging) but loving and accepting.

While these shifts show a reworking and reconstruction of their Christian faith, the faith they describe is a typical, EPC church-based faith.

The other three people in this grouping were all categorised as Wayfinders in the original study. These people had remained participants in church as they worked through significant personal faith changes. The churches they belong to are not typical EPC style churches. One of these people said about doing the study five years later:

> Five years is too short a time for me. I prefer ten years as that's when I started questioning my faith and the church. I looked for others who were doing this too and I found them in the church. Most of us still are – i.e. only three out of 24 of us no longer belong to and regularly attend a church.

These six people demonstrate that churches can retain people who may otherwise have left. They can also provide resources for people to work through core faith changes and crises while continuing to be involved in church.

THE JOURNEY OF THE DISPLACED

Six of the Displaced replied to the questionnaire, representing 31.5% of the Displaced in the original Churchless Faith study. Four had no links with any established church and continued to reflect the faith characteristics of Displaced Followers. Two had become Returnees as they had returned to participation within an established EPC church and exhibited a typical EPC church-based faith similar to that of three of the interviewees discussed above who had not left the established church.

Both of these trajectories were consistent with anticipated paths. They indicate that these people, whether part of an established church or not, remained in a stable EPC faith position. The four Displaced who were not part of an established church nevertheless had ongoing supports to their faith. Three were part of small groups (Bible Study Fellowship [BSF] or other study groups) and the fourth indicated that Christian books and TV programmes were an ongoing support. Interestingly it was this fourth person, Anne-Marie, who had no connection with any group that shared her faith, who showed the greatest indications that she was beginning to question her previously clear EPC faith:

Anne-Marie [I'm] less certain as to the divinity of Jesus Christ, virgin birth and conception . . . more reserved in wanting to make others see things the way I do . . . [and] not so certain that I have answers to all life situations that in earlier life (18-25 years) seemed black and white.

In the original research it was postulated that the Displaced *may* develop questions, doubts and criticisms about their EPC Faith and move towards the position of the Exiles. Although this was suggested, only one interviewee spoke of his faith changing in this way and unfortunately we were not able to contact him as part of the five-year-on follow-up.

To the Displaced group must be added a married couple who were described as Wayfinders in *A Churchless Faith.* When we analysed their questionnaire responses it was clear that they exhibited the faith stances of the Displaced. This posed a problem. Either they had been incorrectly categorised as Wayfinders five years previously or they had moved in their faith position. We concluded it was the former.[14]

Adding these two misplaced Wayfinders to the category of the Displaced brings the total number of Displaced to eight. The faith of the Displaced is consistent in theology and orientation to that of the Returnees. The only difference is that the Returnees are involved in an established church while the Displaced are not. The faith position of both groups is very stable.

From among the group of Displaced identified five years ago, six returned questionnaires. Two had returned to church and four remained outside the institutional expressions of church. For most this had now become a very long-term alienation from established forms of church. It is therefore expected that these Displaced Followers will continue in their faith supported by study groups, TV programmes and books but outside any institutional expression of the faith.

Interestingly the two who had returned to a church had been out of church for a relatively short period of time – less than one year – and their reasons for leaving were very much focused on the leadership style of one particular church. This may indicate that the opportune time to attempt to reintegrate the Displaced into a church community is as soon as possible after leaving. It would appear that the longer they are outside a church, the less likely they are to consider becoming involved again. Obviously this also depends on the degree to which they have been hurt by a specific church or a number of churches. Certainly an argument could be made that the greater the sense of hurt and alienation and the longer the time period out of the church, the less likely they are to consider a return to a church community.

Indications from this sample suggest that the Displaced Followers' faith represents a stable expression of Christian faith. They do not belong to a particular church community; nevertheless they have a committed and clear Christian faith. This faith is nurtured and supported by their involvement in study groups and other faith groups which are not connected to specific churches. A majority of this group mentioned the support they receive from books, seminars and Christian television preachers. They are highly sceptical of churches and their leaders and do not want to be involved in a church community.[15]

WHAT HAPPENED TO THE EXILES?

Eleven of the original group of thirty-two Exiles returned the follow-up questionnaire (34%). Four of the eleven remained in the same or a very similar faith position; three had moved to adopt an alternative faith position (no longer describing themselves as being *Christian* in any sense of the word); three had moved to a Wayfinders faith position; and one had reconnected with an established church and a traditional EPC church-based faith position (Returnee).

This degree of changed faith position (64% of Exiles) shows the crossroads of faith that Exiles encounter. Their faith has entered a very confusing and disorienting phase in which they are busily deconstructing the beliefs and understandings they had been given while they were part of an established EPC church. This process, after five years, has brought the people involved to a place where a variety of outcomes might be equally possible Some, when their faith has been sufficiently deconstructed and they begin to build again for the future, turn in the direction of agnosticism or some expression of 'new age' spirituality. Others create a new expression of Christian faith.

Rachel is a typical Exile. In her questionnaire she speaks of not having a warm image of God and of struggling with coming to God in prayer. She says "God is distant. I'm constantly in awe of his creation – sunrises etc. I don't have a fixed belief . . . ." About God she mentions "a fear and distrust of God" coupled with "a gratefulness that he continues with routines (i.e. sunrises and weekends)." When asked if she has a faith she replies – "Faith? The older I get the less I know is true for me. My faith now is a belief in God and the Trinity, and belief that I am walking in a plan – which is full of choices . . . ." Jesus she sees as a friend.

Rachel says she doesn't read the Bible. She tries now and again and can remember some passages but when she reads them now they don't seem edifying. She has no idea of the purpose of human life and doesn't really have a sense of personally important faith or God experiences. Reflecting on this she states it is "sad when I think about it. I'm in a stage when I'm not quite one thing or another, but a misfit – I guess."

Rachel sums up her present faith stance by saying "I ask myself if I've lost my faith – it was one thing I used to be worried would happen because I used to be so passionate. But I tell myself that God holds me in his hand – and I'm not sure now if that's my hope (as a child hopes) or my definite belief. I don't know where I am faith wise as I have no-one to compare myself with – and I don't know if there is a measurement?" Rachel has tried going back to church but doesn't really fit. She doesn't belong to a faith group but does continue to say grace with meals and sometimes she and the children read the "Radio Rhema word for each day" (a book of daily readings published by a Christian radio station). Looking to the future she says "I feel frightened to ask for help from God. I tend to be a bit gutsier standing up for myself – but would love a few miracles and a bit more passion about my faith."

For Rachel the sense of a wilderness of faith continues. This is a disorienting and painful place. To be in this same place five years later must be very lonely and disheartening.

Another of the Exiles interviewed five years ago is in a very similar place to Rachel but with perhaps some indications of movement in her faith – movement towards the direction of the Explorer faith stance. She claims she does have a faith now and that her faith is much broader than five years ago. Describing her faith she says "I'm not that 'particular' about the trinity. God is God, Jesus was . . . that I'm still working out. The Holy Spirit is anyone's guess." On a number of questions about her faith she says the jury is still out or she is still working things out. For her the main questions are "Who is Jesus Christ? What is the Holy Spirit? And what about the other religions?" There are however indications of movement as she says "I've probably revisited and appreciate some of the things I threw out – e.g. Christmas and Easter."

WHAT HAPPENED TO THE EXPLORERS?

Seven Explorers from the original group of 19 returned questionnaires (37%). Not surprisingly, this group showed a high degree of directional change. This was to be expected because these people were at a transitional point where they were beginning to build a new, autonomous faith.

In two cases there was no change. Both respondents were characterised as holding an Explorer's faith stance with some indications of the Exile's stance. Predominantly, however, they were assessed as Explorers.

Two had moved to a more questioning, less certain and less active faith position (categorised as Exiles). One of these two, Edward, had undergone a substantial geographical, cultural and work shift that had isolated him from many of his friendships and Christian networks. He wrote extensively about this change of faith, lamenting to some degree what he had lost. The other had some involvement for family reasons in a Pentecostal church. This was a church he attended occasionally.

Although attending this church he had a number of major questions about core elements of the Christian faith and was best characterised as an Explorer.

One person who had exhibited signs of an Explorer's faith stance five years ago has since moved back into a Pentecostal church and now holds a faith position best described as a Returnee. The last two Explorers have moved to the faith position expressed by the Wayfinders.

WHAT HAPPENED TO THE ALTERNATIVE FAITH EXPLORERS?

Five of the seven Alternative Faith Explorers responded to the questionnaire. This, the smallest of the groupings, represented the highest percentage questionnaire return rate (71%). All five (100%) remained in an alternative faith position. None had moved in the direction of reinvolvement in Christian faith. One person, as will be discussed below, held to some aspects of a Christian faith. This indicates that the Alternative Faith position is a stable faith category. The following quotes illustrate the faith positions of people who have made a transition to an Alternative Faith.

Alison describes her faith, saying for her:

> God is a word to describe the greatest things in life e.g. love, beauty, truth, creative genius, power, life and to describe the realities of a spiritual non-material world (of which we know very little).

Prayer for Alison is "focusing of spiritual energy and as such sometimes causes things to change – believing strongly creates the energy for positive spiritual things to happen." About Jesus she states he was "a person with exceptional spiritual powers. He is the model of spiritual excellence . . . . His followers unable to accept his death 'saw' him again."

Speaking of how her faith is changing she says "I am moving more and more away from Christian norms each year as I live in today's society and see/know people who are not Christian and who are happy, confident, serving. In comparison the church seems to have a diminutive effect on people's lives."

Jane, who is not part of any faith group, calls herself "a person with spiritual values – not a faith in one Judeo Christian God." She sees "many psychological principles (for good psych health) are intuitively achieved through the ritual of prayer," which she sees as "talking to myself" or "executive functioning".

Julie states that "faith to me is a word with connotations of religion. I believe in a universal 'great spirit' or divine intelligence and so you could call that being a person of faith I guess." Describing a mature faith she says the idea of mature faith still carries "connotations of religion for me. But in its truest sense, someone who has travelled beyond their ego, who is joyful, alive, 'in the flow', and through their being touches, changes or heals."

Russell no longer sees himself as having a faith:

> I feel I have resolved faith questions, and feel happy with my choices. The big step was to finally recognise the idea of God was no longer justifiable or relevant to me. Took a lot of courage to make this step, but felt it was the only honest position I could take.

For Graeme "God is a human construct that exists in the psychological and sociological structures of people's lives. This does not deny its profound meaning or significance however."

WHAT HAPPENED TO THE WAYFINDERS?

This faith grouping had the largest total number of returned questionnaires – thirteen in all.

Twelve of the thirteen Wayfinders were seen as still reflecting the faith stance of Wayfinders five years on, while one was now best described as an Exile.

In addition to these twelve were a number of others who had moved during the five years towards the Wayfinders' faith position. This group includes Lucy, Fiona and Nigel who have over the years between these studies moved in their faith stance from being Exiles to Wayfinders. The following comments from them indicate the kind of faith they have now and their feelings about their faith. These comments are typical of the Wayfinders and demonstrate how these people have moved from the faith of the Exiles described above.

Lucy replies to the question "Would you consider yourself a person of faith today?" by writing "Definitely." She goes on to describe this faith, saying it is "an experiential and intellectual knowledge of the existence of the Creator and a relationship between us based on commitment, love and forgiveness." She describes the components of her faith today as "Love, accountability, acceptance of God's right to be God, the necessity of my staying in an honest relationship with God, making God the centre of my existence."

Prayer for Lucy is a "necessary part of everyday life. [It is] not a separate 'quiet time' or prayer regime but simple chatting going about one's business." Describing her relationship with God, she says she always has important faith/God experiences. "Like my relationship with family members, most of it is mundane day to day stuff and occasionally a great time together and sometimes a need for God to do a 'God thing' in my life. But I need to feel connected to God daily just as I need to interact with my family members."

Lucy is not part of a faith group or church. Commenting on church she says it's "OK for others, it achieved some good things in my life but can't see it has anything of value for me at this stage in my life. But that's not to say the future will exclude some sort of church (I have been out of church for 9 years now). [I] can't face singing all those choruses ad infinitum/listening to the same old stories or sermons."

Fiona and Nigel have made a similar move to Lucy from the faith of the Reflective Exiles to that of Integrated Wayfinders. Both have been part of a faith group and have found this a significant part of their journey. Fiona describes her group as "a small group of 15 families". She goes because she likes "the original and honest way people lead" although her only involvement is having morning tea. Nigel says he goes along to a faith group and calls it his "church".

CONCLUSION

In the table on the next page, the faith stance movement of the 47 people involved in the five-year-on follow-up is shown in comparison to their faith stance in the previous study. The shaded squares indicate no substantial change. For the majority of respondents (68%) there was no substantial shift of faith over the five-year period. This is particularly the case for the Displaced and Returnees (taken together 82% no change), those with an alternative faith (100% no change) and the Wayfinders (90% no change).

The Exiles (36% stable – 64% movement) and Explorers (28% stable – 72% movement) showed greater degrees of faith change over the five-year period. For both the Exiles and the Explorers there was movement in a number of directions. Both groupings showed examples of people who had gone back to an EPC faith stance and reconnected with established churches, and those who had become Wayfinders. Three Exiles moved during the five years away from a Christian-based faith towards an Alternative Faith.

Five Years On

Faith Category original Study	Faith Category – Five Years On					
	Returnees to EPC Church	Displaced	Exiles	Explorers	Alternative Faith Explorers	Wayfinders
Established Church Participation (6)	3					3[16]
Displaced (8)	2	6				
Exiles (11)	1		4		3	3
Explorers (7)	1		2	2		2
Alternative Faith Explorers (5)					5	
Wayfinders (10)			1			9
TOTAL (47)	7	6	7	2	8	17

OUR STUDY'S FINDINGS

3 The Leavers Describe Their Own Faith

THE FOLLOWING CHAPTERS look in some detail at the responses to the questionnaire. There is a sense in which this is very much 'holy ground'. Those people who agreed to take part in the study took the time and the thought to wrestle with their faith, their beliefs and some of their experiences of God, and to try to describe the results. We received these honest, brave and sometimes moving responses with gratitude and respect. While it has been possible to draw out themes common to each group, at the same time we recognise the uniqueness of each person's journey.

The questionnaire invited the respondents to describe their own faith today. Question 1 and part 'a' of question 2 asked "Do you consider yourself a person of faith today? If so how would you describe your faith? What are the key components of it?"[17]

Their responses fall into two major categories:

1. The Returnees, Displaced and Wayfinders saw themselves as strongly and definitely people of faith and were able to describe its nature. While there was a similar strength of conviction among these three groups, their respective understandings of their faith were very different.

2. The faith of the Exiles and Explorers faith was characterised more by questions, doubt and an ongoing process of trying to find a faith that fitted them. Several Alternative Faith Explorers also fitted this category, because if they did describe a faith it tended to be more vaguely apprehended and was lacking in detailed content.

Returnees used conventional EPC church language to describe what were clearly deeply held convictions. The way they described their faith indicated its personal nature and importance for the whole of their lives.

Matthew   I believe that Jesus Christ is Lord of my life.

Graeme   A deeper relationship with the Father, Son and Holy Spirit. A more relaxed personal relationship.

These Returnees tended to describe their faith quite briefly using traditional language:

Delwyn [View of God is] Biblical! We remain about the same [as 5 years ago]. No salvation without Jesus Christ and no power to live the Christian life without the Holy Spirit.

Although no longer involved in a church the Displaced expressed a similar faith. Six of the seven included the words "no change" or "the same" in their description of their faith. This indicated that they did not perceive any changes in their faith since I had interviewed them five years previously. They described a 'personal faith' emphasising the role of the Father, Son and Holy Spirit as well as the Bible.

Gwyn   Faith based on God's word outworking in personal experience of his keeping faithfulness and incredible love toward me. Personal relationship with God and Jesus, leading of Holy Spirit, acceptance and embracing of all scripture.

The Displaced describe God with terms like "creator", "father", "awesome", "powerful" and "loving".

Laura God is sovereign and in control. [Jesus and the Holy Spirit] are part of the Trinity as expressed in the Bible. Jesus is the way to the Father and the Holy Spirit is the comforter . . . .

Darren Jesus remains my closest friend.

Some expressed some tension between what they believed and what they were personally experiencing. One wrote "God is . . . a loving Father but sometimes my experiences of my earthly Dad cloud this view."

Others indicated some doubt or questioning around elements of their faith package:

Simon Jesus – not sure.

Darren Not sure about where the Holy Spirit fits in.

Anne-Marie [God is] a Spirit linking all humanity. A creative force which continues to shape the universe. [The] Holy Spirit [is] within each person, like a battery charger. See the Holy Spirit as a well which releases the waters throughout life allowing us to overcome difficulties. Less certain as to the Divinity of Jesus Christ – virgin birth and conception.

In Anne-Marie's statement we see evidence of some questioning of core elements of her faith. There are indications in this of a move towards the faith stance of the Reflective Exiles.

The faith of the Returnees and the Displaced can be contrasted with that of the Wayfinders. Although the latter also strongly affirmed their faith using words like "definitely" and "absolutely" and drew on clearly Christian concepts, they went on to describe a more dynamic, open and integrated faith.

Unlike the groups above they used dynamic language and vocabulary to describe their faith, choosing words like "discover", "journey", "growing", "openness", "work out", "fluid", "changing". Michelle, for example, spoke of having "a range of beliefs held in tension/unison = paradox."

Their faith expressed an openness and breadth:

Melanie I am a Christian but on a journey where rules, regulations, formulae are irrelevant. I'm comfortable saying that my faith journey is about growing in understanding of God, myself, and other people but don't wish to define it much beyond that.

Their faith is integrally connected with their lives:

Denis Faith is certainly still the basis of my daily life, world view and journeying. It is Christo-centric, lived in the now/not yet nature of the Kingdom of God. It is characterised by comfort, security, scrutiny and challenge.

Notice again the paradoxical nature of the faith that Denis describes as he links the words comfort and challenge, security and scrutiny.

It strikes us that most, probably all, of these people would affirm the old statement: 'I believe fewer things now, but what I do believe I hold far more firmly than I once did.'

The Wayfinders expressed specifically Christian theology. They describe God as "loving", as "Creator", as "personal", as "a God of grace", as "indwelling all things", as "good, patient and forgiving". They describe Jesus as the "Son of God", as "revealing God", as "equal with God", "the God man". They describe the Holy Spirit as "God's agent", as "present and pervasive", as "resident in believers", as "equal with God", as "part of the Godhead".[18]

What distinguishes the Wayfinders is not so much the content of their beliefs as the way they express them. Most of them describe God from a context of God-ly experience:

Wayne I see God as . . . directing and encouraging.

Melanie God is at the centre of the way I relate to life

Bill I believe God is for me, encouraging, warning, enabling me . . . .

Many Wayfinders use language that shows they consider themselves to have a developing understanding of God:

Melanie God continues to get 'bigger', but remains personal, loving and at the centre of the way I interpret/relate to life.

Nicola God becomes larger, more awesome, yet I feel closer, more intimate.

Here we sense something of the way that these people's experience of God, like that of the Old Testament character Job, has become both much bigger and at the same time more personal and intimate. Many express the sense of God's being a mystery.

Michelle My view of God . . . . Big, beyond-gender, beyond-culture, beyond-time. I feel at times awed, silenced, frightened, doubting, curious, fascinated, distanced, warm . . . towards God.

Several Wayfinders have reflected deeply on the nature of God, and some have undertaken theological study. Some make a point of using untraditional language to describe their idea of God. For example, Michelle's statement continues:

Michelle I have difficulty with the term 'God'. I think of 'Spirit', or 'Other' or 'Essence' . . . in fact, anything but the names/titles I used to use. Not that they don't have meaning . . . for many, but they are too loaded with prescriptive meaning for me, too saturated with aspects of church culture which I've come to find restrictive, suffocating, limiting . . . I've needed new language for my relationship with God. I especially can't handle the 'him' and 'her' thing . . . not because I'm rabidly feminist, but because these titles/words are so limiting.

Or consider the depth and poetry of Denis:

Denis God is Wisdom Worker, Meaning Giver, Providential Guider, Sufferer of all suffering . . . .

This does not mean that the Integrated Wayfinders don't also struggle with aspects of who God is.

Nigel On the one hand I (rationally) see him as a God of boundless love. But I also (at a deeper, subconscious level) see him as unaccepting and vindictive.

It would not be fair to conclude that Wayfinders have a more dynamic Christian faith than Returnees or Displaced believers. But certainly the way they describe their beliefs indicates that Wayfinders have a much more conscious habit of reflection, not only on their belief, but on their experience. They describe an organic faith, a faith which is growing and changing. Perhaps ironically, Returnees and the Displaced are much more prone to mention a 'personal relationship' with God or Jesus Christ, yet it is the Wayfinders who actually describe what sounds like a personal relationship. In doing so, they use active verbs in contrast to static nouns.

This is quite different from the Exiles and Explorers. Their faith descriptions are characterised more by questions, they have few certainties and less talk of a personal connection with God. Where the Exiles and Explorers differ is the sense the Explorers have of an ongoing process of faith involving an increasing clarity of faith content. Compare, for example, Rachel (an Exile) and Explorers Dianne and Lynne.

Rachel Faith? The older I get the less I know is true for me. My faith now is a belief in God . . . I'm not passionate about my faith as I was . . . God is distant.

Dianne Yes I do [have a faith. It is] deep, changing, very open.

Lynne I think that some of the things about God that I hardly dared hope were true (i.e. things I wanted him to be) are firming up into realities, slowly and surely.

Dianne goes on to explain that her faith includes belief in God, the Son of God, resurrection and heaven and hell.

The Exiles, describing their faith, use the words "I don't know". Where God is characterised he is often seen as distant. There are more questions than answers for this group, even confusion at times. None of this group sees Jesus as divine:

Ruth Jesus Christ – was he really God? I no longer 100% agree. A radical theologian for his time. He pointed the way to God.

Robert I lean towards a benevolent God. Have trouble believing he would toss the majority into a fiery hell . . . I seem to have lost touch with Jesus . . . but believe in the hand of the Holy Spirit upon me.

Rachel [admits to contradictions in her view of God] . . . fear and distrust of God. But a gratefulness that he continues with routines like sunrise and weekends . . . Jesus – the friend. Holy Spirit able to work in people's minds . . . I guess [I have] an element of trust in God's awesomeness – which doesn't equate with what I said above about God.

The Explorers tended to describe movement over the five years towards a greater sense of understanding of God.

Lynne I find it much easier to see him/her [God] as exciting, 'liberated'(!) and acting outside the square.

Dianne [I'm] not so narrow-minded about my views of God. [Jesus Christ and the Holy Spirit are both still] real and active.

The Alternative Faith Explorers did not talk of specific Christian content to their faith. Five of the eight said they were agnostic and now had no faith in any supernatural being. The remaining three talked of a generalised belief in a "higher being" or "divine intelligence".

Jane [I am] a person of spiritual values. Not faith in one Judeo-Christian God.

Jenny Yes [I am a person of faith]. Much broader and not linked to any doctrine or religious set of guidelines. A general belief in a Higher Power of spiritual realm beyond the physical.

Neil I do not consider myself a person of faith.

The Alternative Faith Explorers tended to describe Jesus as either as a model of the spiritual life or as "simply a man" around whom much has been made up in subsequent years. This group did not see Jesus in any way as God:

Russell God is a human construct that exists in the psychological and sociological structures of people's lives. This does not deny its profound meaning or significance however

. . . Jesus was simply a man around whom legends and myths were established.

Alison God is not a personal being. God is a concept to describe spiritual realities. My image to embody spiritual values is a loving and powerful female being . . . . Jesus was a person with exceptional spiritual powers. He is the model of spiritual excellence . . . .

4 The Bible, Human Nature, Evangelism and Mission

THE BIBLE

People's view of the Bible linked strongly with their descriptions of their own beliefs about God, Jesus and the Holy Spirit. The Returnees and Displaced see the Bible as "the Word of God", as significant, important and authoritative. Laura and Anne-Marie (both Displaced) are typical of that group in describing their understanding:

> *Laura* The Bible clearly states that God is the Word and the word is God. It is the core of our faith.

> *Anne-Marie* [The Bible is] our insight into the nature of God.

Exiles see the Bible in quite different terms. For them it is not a divine book. It does not hold the status and authority that the previous two groups give it. Although some recalled a time in their lives when it meant much more to them, the Reflective Exiles see the Bible as a 'good book' rather than as 'The Word of God'.

> *Robert* The Bible used to have a black and white answer to every question. Frankly I struggle to be inspired by it these days.

> *Ruth* A good book – full of history, theology of the time and . . . that's about it.

Those who are Alternative Faith Explorers would agree that the Bible is a significant historical text and that it is a very human document. For them it certainly is not the word of God. Despite this, several expressed appreciation for certain aspects of it – "contains great metaphors", "good teachings, lyrical poetry", "contains many powerful, substantial all-time truths". Perhaps Neil sums it up when he says:

> A subjective historical book with all the flaws and mistakes of any book written years ago . . . .

Explorers, on the other hand, have a cautiously positive approach to the Bible. While they are clear that it can't be taken literally but rather needs to be interpreted, they go on to recognise a place for it in their own faith.

> *Dianne* I believe that [the Bible] still has a part in our lives today. You can't take it literally.

> *Lynne* I'm less keen to ignore it but I think a lot of knowledge and thought is required for its correct interpretation.

The Wayfinders value the Bible as a record or source document. They are clear that while they value it they don't regard it in the way they used to: "still precious, less magical". Several use phrases like "the Word of God" and "inspired" but with careful qualifications:

> *Stuart* It contains the inspired word of God but all bits are not equally inspired and God's living word is much greater than the scripture, important as that is.

> *Tim* True in all it plainly affirms of the nature of God, man, sin. It is a record of salvation history but it's not to be held in awe – God is. In the past I've sometimes looked to the pages of scripture for the truth – now I tend to look more to the events/ theology/insights written about within its pages.

> *Nigel* I see the Bible as inspired by God, but not God's literal words, and probably not inerrant.

Some Wayfinders read the Bible regularly, some occasionally, some very little. Two mentioned that having spent a long period of time not reading the Bible has enabled them to approach it with fresh appreciation. Some Wayfinders could be described as comfortably ambiguous about the Bible. They find parts of it very helpful and regard other parts as an enigma, or completely irrelevant. They have doubts about just what kind of book it is or claims to be, but the doubts don't bother them. Bill, who has thought intensively about this, wrote:

> *Bill* I spent most of one year wrestling with the question of what the Bible actually is – the Word of God or not? and what does that mean anyway? I came to believe it has clear signs of deficiency . . . and do not believe it was dictated by God. However as a record of the faith journey of God's people it is indispensable and invaluable to us. And as that record it IS in a sense God's word and speaks to us like no other book . . . . I find my position now both peaceful and powerful – I don't have to try and pretend there are no errors or contradictions in the Bible . . . but I can nonetheless let it speak authoritatively to me. It's great!

HUMAN NATURE

When asked about human nature and the purpose of life, the Returnees and the Displaced saw the purpose of life to be in relationship with God. They saw human nature as "sinful" or "fallen", but with the possibility of redemption through Christ.

Exiles are very unsure about both. They say they "have no idea", they "struggle with this question" or that humans are a mix of good and evil. The Explorers were not unified in their response. One saw human nature as "very precious", one as "sinful in parts". Helen had the clearest perspective:

> *Helen* I believe in the fall, and our ultimate redemption. I believe that Jesus paid that price on the cross. We are here to learn to be more Christ-like, to become more patient, enduring, selfless etc.

The Alternative Faith Explorers responded to this question with comments like "who knows", "not sure". Some, like Russell, were more definite:

Russell Humans *make* our own purpose though we do not do it alone. We create meaning with social relationships . . . . Humans are creative and culture evolves. Even if we agree there is a *true* meaning to life this is an impossible thing to prove . . . . All that said, perhaps love (agape in particular) is not a bad view of human purpose.

Alison Humans inherit the potential for both good and evil. Because of a very strong bent towards the need for social acceptance plus the process of socialising and humans' ability to identify with others. Most people are good. The purpose of life is none – each person makes their own.

More than the other groups, a majority of Wayfinders spoke of the goodness inherent in human nature. Humans are "weak" and "imperfect" but can be seen as "basically good rather than basically evil."

Nigel I used to hold to the common evangelical view that human nature is basically evil, but doing a theology paper made me seriously question that belief.

Human weakness is seen as inviting God's compassion and forgiveness rather than judgement or punishment. A number of Wayfinders describe the purpose of life in terms of getting "to know God", "to find God and be in relationship with God", or to "bring glory to God". At the same time they seem to have a sense that the purpose of life involves "knowing oneself", "becoming oneself", "being responsible for one's own behaviours", "loving others", "doing 'good works' for which God created us". As Denis says, the two are interrelated – "The purpose of human life is to constantly discover the life God gives in Christ and to devote oneself to it".

Michelle All life is sacred; [I] have a lot of respect for the created world. People are amazing – great capacity for marvellous heights – and horrendous depths. Increasingly see Life in people's woundedness/lack of wholeness/weakness. My concepts of what it is to be 'successful' have changed a lot. Overall, I see our purpose as human beings to reflect Glory and bring pleasure to him/her.

EVANGELISM AND MISSION

The Returnees and Displaced seem to take mission for granted. It is part of their faith and something which arises naturally out of faith.

> *Sonia* [Mission is] important – obviously a basic call on the life of a Christian. I am not an evangelist so I try to live my life as a Christian and let that do the talking. Something I continually struggle with as to what I should be doing.

Some are passionate about sharing their faith. Steve, for example, claims to be "sharing my faith more now than five years ago." Others, like Linda, are less passionate about sharing her faith than five years ago.

> *Laura* My driving motivation is to help others know and have faith in the word of God (Bible) to be equipped in all of life's circumstances. [I] have several non-Christian friends and share with them on appropriate occasions.

> *Anne-Marie* [I] believe that every life has value and needs to be treated with respect. More reserved in wanting to make others see things the way I do.

The Exiles have little enthusiasm for mission and few saw a connection between their faith and their community involvement. None have any interest in sharing their faith. That is if they still have a faith – something which several disclaim.

> *Rachel* To be able to 'give something back' is important. Whether faith is the impetus – I haven't thought about that one. I'm more comfortable talking about my spiritual side – because it's unique to me. I don't have a mission but I'll sometimes encourage others to talk about their spiritual side.

> *Robert* Without my faith I doubt whether I would care too much about these things [wider community action or service]. I used to feel I was Billy Graham's right hand man. I doubt if I have shared my faith in the last five years.

Edward Faith is not the impetus. If there is something that I see as helping those in need I may contribute . . . . What faith do I have to share?

The Explorers wrote of a general compassion and willingness to help others but also remained reluctant about the idea of sharing their faith.

Helen [On sharing faith] I don't. I'm so unsure of what I can really rely on god for when it comes down to it – apart from heaven-when-I-get-there. I can't share my faith enthusiastically when I haven't seen Scriptural promises come true in the way that I had been taught they would be.

Those who have moved away from Christian faith towards an alternative faith stance rejected the notion that their involvement in helping others could be linked to their faith. As one said: "my involvement in service is because of being a human, not a Christian. (Humans innately love and serve others)." Again none of the group who have moved towards a non-Christian based faith wants to 'convert' people. For them "it is more important to have respect for other's paths". Alison summed up this feeling:

Alison Sharing things that are important is natural. If it's a requirement it's false. Sharing must be in context that what you believe is good for you but the other person's situation/ needs etc. are different.

The Wayfinders have a broad and varied perspective on how or whether their faith makes an impact on their involvement with the world. A few disclaimed any impact. The majority saw service as growing out of their faith. Wayne said, "My faith is just who I am so my involvement with others is an expression of who I am." This affected his work practices and ethics. Geoff said mission is expressed "in doing my job well". Three spoke explicitly of a sense of God's presence in their vocational work. When it comes to 'mission', several spoke of sharing their faith but with the proviso that the culture of others should be respected, beliefs should never be imposed on others and faith can't be communicated as a "finished package". Proselytising was not their main purpose.

A number seem comfortable about sharing their faith verbally, in the right situation and without being self conscious. Lucy wrote of sharing her faith: "As opportunities present themselves. Also sometimes [I] enhance these perceived opportunities. [It is] important to share Truth about life."

Stuart feels similarly: "Friendship evangelism is genuine friendship first and evangelism second. I really like the post-modern environment where spirituality can be discussed more openly." Julian wrote "I am uncomfortable with the proselytising of some people of faith. I try to be an example of my beliefs and values, but I do not deliberately avoid discussing these things. I will happily refer to God, my faith and the like in conversation where it is appropriate." Others preferred to encourage people to "explore spirituality" or to share their faith "primarily through just being".

> *Nicola*   I concentrate on doing/being my unique self and trust that out of this will come effective service, action and "sharing" of my faith . . . through my daily life, meeting people, being the best 'me' I can be.

5 Prayer and Personal Faith Experiences

"WHAT IS PRAYER FOR YOU? What do you feel is happening when you pray?" These two questions invited people to reflect on what part, if any, prayer played in their lives five years on.

The Returnees and Displaced saw prayer as essential to their faith and life. They spoke of prayer as communication with God, a communication that God hears. Results and answers were also important parts of prayer. Typical perspectives from the Returnees included:

> *Delwyn* God is interested in every part of our lives and it's a joy to have fellowship with him.

> *Samantha* Through Jesus' blood I can now draw near to God. God knows my needs and others'. God hears when I pray.

And from the Displaced:

> *Darren* Prayer is a cornerstone of my relationship with God . . . . I feel I am talking directly to God as friend/Father.

> *Anne-Marie* Prayer is very important. Never left unheard. [Prayer is] acknowledgement of God, confirms beliefs. Opens pathways to see and experience God's love.

Prayer for the Exiles becomes an occasional thing. This is a major difference from the two groups above who saw prayer as essential. Rosemary speaks of prayer as an "occasional conversation [during which] nothing much is happening." Another saw prayer as "great/

51

essential" but his "own application is fitful". When Exiles pray it is less for answers than for the sense of being in God's presence:

> *Robert* For me prayer keeps open a line to God . . . . Prayer helps to keep me aware of God and his goodness and keeps my conscience sharpened.

> *Ruth* I hadn't realised how many 'asks' my prayer contained. I still pray from time to time but it's more for me to accept life in all its wholeness . . . I get a greater sense of how big this world is, how time, nature, changing theology, is just part of the world and us.

The Explorers struggled with prayer. Two of the three said they didn't pray. One said it is "a powerful and direct link to God. But I don't do it." Another described prayer as "God coming into a situation."

The people on the Alternative Faith spectrum were divided in their perspective on prayer. One group, those people who had moved to a generalised faith in some kind of spiritual being(s), spoke of prayer as engagement with spiritual energies.

> *Alison* Prayer is a focusing on spiritual reality symbolised by a 'God' or 'Goddess' image. It is a tapping into a universal energy to cause things to happen, and it is a time of perspective and truth.

> *Julie* [Prayer is] being a channel for a purer intelligence.

Those who have moved to agnosticism saw prayer as meditation, reflection or personality development but did not link this with a divine being. They did, however, value its positive psychological effects.

> *Russell* Don't pray in traditional sense. But has value in meditation, can help self awareness . . . . The conservative view that believes prayer makes/causes God to act is foolish and egocentric.

> *Heather* [Prayer is] mind stilling/re-orienting time. I don't [pray] in any sense that involves 'the other'.

All the Wayfinders affirmed the reality of God and the value of prayer. In this sense they have much in common with the Returnees and the Displaced. They differed in that the Wayfinders responded at much greater length and described prayer in quite different terms. Their responses not only indicated that they were pray-ers but demonstrated that they had reflected personally about the nature of prayer.

For the Wayfinders, prayer is an ongoing part of daily life although they may also pray at specific times. A few mentioned the value of liturgical or set prayers. They described it as "a continuing conversation", "an attitude of life", "listening, awareness, being open to life". Several of them described prayer as a mystery, yet within this mystery they have a sense of a compassionate listener whom they can trust, whatever the 'results' of their prayers may be.

Prayer is about personal connection and deep relationship. They spoke of "relationship building", an "expression of intimacy", "a sense of being held", "a sense of oneness with God". Furthermore, prayer not only allows contact with God but also enables the "true self to grow". "Prayer," says one Wayfinder, "is seeking to be moved into the place where I can truly be who I truly am."

Many Wayfinders wanted to develop or grow in prayer and in fact this group's main desire in prayer appears to be a greater sense of God's purpose in their lives. For all of the Integrated Wayfinders, prayer seems to be less about specific requests and more about bringing themselves and the people or situations that concern them into God's presence or light.

The following comments from respondents give some feeling for their perspective on prayer.

> *Stuart* Prayer is not simply a spiritual exercise. There are no sacred/secular distinctions . . . . Prayer for others is actually a reaching out to others (as well as to God) and in some way grasping them by the shoulders and giving love to them . . . . Prayer is about 'connectedness'.

> *Nicola* Prayer is my/our/church's communication with God. A continuing conversation with our heavenly Father. Something to do all day as well as at special times and on special days. I feel exposed before God when I pray, so have

to be honest . . . but trying to be transparent I do feel 'heard' and have the real sense of supporting others when I pray for them.

Mark [Prayer is] more relationship building, say, than changing events through prayers . . . . A sense of one-ness with God, being transported to another space. A remembering of who I am and who God is.

Denis My spirituality is predominantly contemplative in mode. All moments are lived in the presence of the immanent/transcendent God. Communion with God involves times of adoration, thanks, confession and intercession.

PERSONAL FAITH EXPERIENCES

Two questions were used to assess people's ongoing experience of faith and the symbols and rituals that continue to hold currency for them. The questions were: "Do you have personally important faith/God experiences now? Are there any religious rituals or symbols that are important to you now? Has their importance changed for you over the last five years?"

The Returnees and Displaced[19] indicate that they continue to have faith experiences but in general do not describe the kind of experiences they have. Some mention communion, scripture and talking to friends. Two gave a little more detail:

Laura Yes I am very conscious of his care and provision for me . . . not based on 'airy-fairy' feelings but on previous knowledge of God through his word. Because my feelings are so unpredictable due to grief I can only rely on what God has said in his word and how he has led me in the past.

Darren [said that Easter had grown in significance and] the image of Christ on a cross is very important to me.

The Exiles did not have continuing experiences of God or faith and did not make use of symbols and rituals.

Ruth   Not like five years ago. I . . . no longer look to God for healing or even to my past sins for repentance. My experiences are small and blend into my life rather than stand out in my life.

Rachel   Not really . . . sad when I think about it. I'm in a stage when I'm not quite one thing or another – but a misfit – I guess I'm grateful when things happen – very grateful – but have no expectations of God whereas when I was younger – I was quite demanding . . . and had positive results . . . . It just doesn't happen for me . . . .

In contrast all the Explorers said they had continued God/faith experiences but were tentative about their nature. The Explorers also had more to say about the role of symbols and rituals for them today. They mentioned specific celebrations like birthdays and Christmas as well as communion and the use of candles. Helen, for example, records a change from five years ago when others had God experiences all the time and she felt second class for not having them. Now, she says "I experience some synchronicity which takes me by pleasant surprise . . . ."

Neil   Not often. I have much closer relationships with others now and I see God in these. I see his love and provision for me mostly expressed this way now.

Most Alternative Faith Explorers gave an unequivocal 'no' to the question of personally important God experiences. One wrote of sometimes experiencing a peace that was in tune with the divine; another spoke of tapping into a spiritual energy. Again, most don't have personally important symbols and rituals. One said no to the question, but then went on to say that at times religious symbols deeply touched him "but not for any objective meaning they represent but rather for a subjective experience they might provoke." He went on to further explain that the life and parables of Jesus, the sayings of Buddha and modern figures like Martin Luther King and Nelson Mandela continued to inspire him.

The Wayfinders continue to have meaningful faith experiences but describe these and their significance in varying ways:

> *Denis*   My daily moment by moment life is lived in a place of resonance with God. This 'resonance' has different tones at times. Adoration, scrutiny, challenge, Shalom.

More cautious responses came from one who claimed "none that are reliable/objective" and another who has a sense on occasion that "it might well be God at work rather than emphatically believing it *must* have been his work". Another doesn't seek faith experiences, finding them 'unhelpful' to faith; but does sense renewed closeness to God at annual retreats.

Most Wayfinders mentioned one or more examples of ritual and symbols which have importance for them. Communion is most commonly named but others included meditation, rosary, crucifix, paintings, use of body positions (kneeling for example), and candles. One spoke of being desensitised to the old Pentecostal icons of the dove, tongues of fire and crosses but finding symbolic importance in personal symbols like her wedding ring.

6 Image of Mature Faith and Personal Growth

"WHAT IS YOUR IMAGE OF A MATURE FAITH?" This section considers the respondents' answers to this question and then sets this alongside their responses to questions about how they feel they are growing, changing and learning.

The Returnees described a mature faith as one exhibiting certain key qualities – loving, sensitive, caring, compassionate, giving, providing, beneficial and positive.

> *Sonia* [A mature faith is] faith and trust in God even when I don't see things working out. This comes through going though life and maturing. Ironically, even though a mature faith it relates to a childlike faith – complete trust.

The Displaced saw mature faith in similar terms. A person exhibiting maturity is described as "someone who has died to self, with the fullness of Christ in their lives"; one who "listens to the Holy Spirit"; or one who is living a life of "balance in all the spiritual disciplines".

> *Laura* [Faith is] tested through trials and proven by standing firm. Based on facts and decisions, *not* feelings.

> *Anne-Marie* [Mature faith is] deep centred belief in God's existence and that all things are working together for good.

Some of the Exiles responded to the question about mature faith by saying "don't know", "I wish I knew" and "as confused as ever". Others provided more clarity:

Rachel   I've had this thought that the more someone gets like Jesus the easier it is to relate to them. I think mature faith is being comfortable with your own faith. I really don't know any answer to this one. Is there such a thing as mature faith? Isn't it constantly discovering new stuff about God and yourself?

Rosemary   [Mature faith is] people happy with their place in God and non-judgmental. Pure motives.

Ruth   [Mature faith is] a faith that doesn't have to justify itself or 'win' people to it. Something that is contented and relaxed.

In contrast to the Displaced and Returnees, the Explorers saw mature faith as being able to live with unanswered questions. Lynne sees a mature faith as "one that can ask hard questions and live with the 'I don't knows' . . . [a faith that is] in touch with real life".

The Alternative Faith Explorers spoke of "personal authenticity", "honesty", "broad perspectives", "responsibility", "tolerance". God was not mentioned as part of their perspective of a mature faith.

Russell   [Mature faith is] perhaps a person who draws inspiration from their tradition, who sees the relativity of faith (sees it embedded in culture) who transcends their own faith boundaries by seeking to dialogue and learn from others' faiths [and] from all who seek to deepen their lives in a more honest and authentic way.

Alison   A mature faith recognises individuality – there is not one answer for all. It accepts the opposing truths in life. It is based on love, not law. It is life affirming, honest and reality based.

The Wayfinders' description of mature faith showed a clear interconnected and relational quality. They describe mature faith in terms of attitudes to God, to oneself, to other people and to 'the world' or the 'reality of daily life'. While for Wayfinders, individuality and personal authenticity are clearly part of this concept of maturity, far more than any of the other groups they express maturity in relational terms. They talk about "participation in the world", "can help others", "accepting self and others", "delights in others' journey", "love, respect and acceptance of others". Some think of maturity as having a sense of the purpose of God in the whole of life and of being aware of one's place in history, family or society.

For Wayfinders, mature faith "has won personal battles" but is confident and stable. It is "not being imposed upon nor imposing on others". It has a broad perspective, "delights in others' journey and questions" and accepts that "there are few black and white answers"; yet recognises the work and presence of the Holy Spirit "wherever and however, especially outside the boxes".

Several Wayfinders talk of faith continuing to develop and change:

> *Michelle*   I live my life in an open, loving and thoughtful manner . . . . As I mature in faith I hope to see this happen more clearly, with less clutter, less resistance to myself and others/Other.

> *Julian*   Each of us has a different faith so . . . what they look like when they mature is going to be different. For me, I think it's about reverence towards God . . . and love, respect and acceptance toward the people I encounter . . . I don't think there is a mature faith (in the singular) any longer.

> *Denis* Mature faith moves though suffering, doubt, questions and disappointments because it is pulled along by a love that enables these to be transformed into an understanding of life, wisdom for the journey, an expanding picture of God and the impetus to contribute to the lives of others.

> *Fiona*   Mature faith is sure of less and less but stronger. I feel my faith has got pared down to the basics of God loves me and I love him.

FAITH GROWTH AND CHANGE

"Where do you feel that you are growing, changing or struggling with faith questions or doubt at the present time? Has this changed in any way over the last five years?

Image of Mature Faith and Personal Growth

"Are there other supports to your faith that are significant to you now? For example: books, magazines, spiritual direction, retreats, seminars, courses, TV or radio programmes?"

This second set of questions allowed us to compare the respondents' view of mature faith and their own sense of personal faith change and growth. It was possible to create a phrase summing up the faith description of each group of respondents.

Grouping of Interviewees	Description of Faith
Returnees	An individual faith
Displaced	A defended faith
Exiles	A doubtful faith
Explorers	A thoughtful faith
Alternative Faith Explorers	A faith without God
Wayfinders	A faith that connects

The Returnees sense a continued growth in their faith. Their descriptions of this change show they are experiencing "personal growth", "personal holiness", and day to day growth in their "personal faith". Their growth is focused on their individual sense of relationship with God, one which affects their attitudes and behaviour. They mention Bible study groups, discussion with other Christians, books, Christian radio and TV programmes, tapes and CDs of Christian music as significant supports to their faith.

Several of the Displaced picture their faith as a house in which to live. Their faith is solid, but they feel it to be sometimes under attack.

Laura My faith in God is solid. I have to believe that He is good ... but I am bewildered and confused by loss. I feel cheated and hurt by God, but still convinced of his working in my life.

Anne-Marie Belief in God has not faltered.

Gwyn I am firmer in my convictions and no longer struggle with the call of God on my life but do struggle sometimes with spiritual opposition directed particularly in the area of my mind. God unbelievably provides strength and I'm really allowing him to build character in me.

The Displaced mentioned books and magazines, some TV programmes (Charles Stanley's is mentioned in particular), study groups, a 'Ha Yesod course' and other Christian Zionist materials, and the Renovare work book and study group as significant supports to their faith.

In contrast the Exiles expressed questions rather than convictions.

Rachel I ask myself if I've lost my faith – it was the one thing I used to be worried would happen because I used to be so passionate. But I tell myself that God holds me in his hand – and I'm not sure now if that's my hope (as a child hopes) or my definite belief. I don't know where I am faith-wise as I have no one to compare myself with – and I don't know if there is a measurement.

Rosemary said she was "finally being honest about what I've thought about for years but because of fear of God/man I was too afraid to be honest". The Reflective Exiles don't name any regular supports to faith.[20]

The Explorers were thoughtful about their faith and their continuing to grapple with key questions. One spoke of the "randomness of life", another of "homosexuality" and the third spoke of the church's inability to meet people's real needs. They spoke of the importance of books in their searching. One also mentioned spiritual direction and poetry as key resources.

The Alternative Faith Explorers described growth in terms of their personal self-confidence. God was not part of this growth. Two spoke of their growth as a direct move away from their previous religious beliefs:

Neil I feel I'm growing slowly towards developing my abilities and accepting my humanity . . . . Religious faith does not come into it.

Alison I am moving more and more away from Christian norms each year as I live in today's society and see/know people who are not Christians and who are happy, confident, serving. In comparison the church seems to have a diminutive effect on people's lives.

Julie [I am] challenged to gather self-belief and power so I can be an agent of change and make a difference in my own life. In my experience religion worked in the opposite way for me, caused a lessening of taking responsibility.

Some Alternative Faith Explorers say they have nothing that supports their faith. Others mentioned friends, books, music, natural beauty and human creativity. One went further, speaking of "meditation retreats, being in love, spiritual teacher/mentor".

A majority of Wayfinders feel their growing edge is in living out their faith in ordinary life. They talked of working out their faith in their marriage and family life and in their Christian community, and of "seeing God's life become a daily reality", discovering "how to outwork" a meaningful contribution to the world; asking "how am I doing life?" Clearly they are continuously evaluating themselves and reflecting on how authentically they are doing in their daily practice of their faith.

The Wayfinders seem comfortable with asking questions, and they take it for granted that change and growth will occur:

Rob I have increasingly gained confidence to ask questions I once feared to allow myself even to consider. Where once I thought I was backsliding I now realise I am growing as I should.

Michelle I continue to struggle and, I believe, to grow . . . . I'm always evaluating my stand, my thoughts and my feelings as issues arise [with my adolescent son.] I'm much less sure of many things than I used to be, but what I am sure of I feel quietly solid about. I struggle/am challenged with how to 'live my life well'. How to be fully me, fully alive. How to love more . . . .

The Wayfinders mention a variety of helps and supports to their faith including:

- Books by a large variety of authors (some clearly Christian, others clearly not)
- Music (classical, Christian and unspecified)
- Friends
- Magazines (*Reality* and *Stimulus*[21] specifically mentioned)
- Courses (Meyers Briggs mentioned)
- Retreats
- Services – specifically Taizé/Celtic
- Psycho-drama; psycho-therapy; counselling
- Spiritual direction
- Creation, works of art, radio.

> *Michelle*   I have to be careful to keep feeding my spirit, which I do by talking with others, (friends, acquaintances or in a fortnightly discussion group) and by reading/contemplation. I enjoy reading Henri Nouwen's words . . . . and am always reading other books which are not overtly Christian but are definitely full of goodness and wisdom.

Compared to the Returnees and Displaced the Wayfinders have a much broader range of sources from which they draw nourishment and support. This group is clearly drawing on both Christian and other sources.

7 Church and Leadership

THE QUESTIONS ON CHURCH WERE INTERPRETED in a number of ways. Some spoke of the ideal church, others of the institutional church and others of their personal experience of church. This variety of interpretations makes analysis difficult. What was universally clear amongst all groups was a negative reaction to at least some church leaders.

All the Returnees affirmed the "need" for a church. Sonia for example called it "God's plan for Christian fellowship". They value a church which is "warm and accepting" and they appreciate being part of a "wider spiritual body", a church which is "family-like [with] sound teaching, worship". The range of views is illustrated by two comments:

> *Delwyn* [Church is] inward looking, mostly motivated by ego-centrical leadership who have their own kingdom-building agendas.

> *Matthew* [admits the church is] anachronistic, struggling to adjust . . . can be a place of misunderstanding, hypocrisy and hurt [but sees it still as] a warm place of resource for participants. I see the need to stick it out especially with people who care but still occasionally hurt each other.

All the Displaced seem to have a reasonably clear idea of what they think church 'should' be and an equally clear conviction that church is not coming up to this standard. Four have strongly negative comments – it "does not meet real needs", "it has lost its way", "it has too much of man, not much of God", it is too "authoritarian in nature".

Church and Leadership

All but one of the Displaced identify themselves as part of some sort of a group of Christian believers. These include Bible Study Fellowships, study groups (connected with a church which the respondent doesn't attend), a Renovare group, a weekly home meeting with like-minded friends. One has begun to experiment with occasionally attending a "raw, unsophisticated, real church" and speaks positively about this experience.

> *Darren* Still struggling with the outworking of formal church (established church). In five years I have tried to belong to a number of churches . . . . We have a weekly group at our home – this group was formed with friends who were not part of an established church or who were not experiencing the depth they/we required from such an established church.

Three Exiles no longer attend any church or faith group, one does so rarely, one has chosen to attend again but finds it a struggle.

> *Rachel* I struggle with the church. I've attended a Baptist Church again this past year – because of the need to belong – but apart from the singing and a few thoughts to take away from the sermon – well – I find there's other 'clubs' I get more of a buzz from.

Other comments include "the jury is still out". The church is "just another corporation" or "a social club" and one person saw the church as a "dangerous breeding ground for neurotics".

Despite these strong negative comments there are also hints of nostalgia for something the church can or once did provide.

The three Explorers divided on this question. One person was not as negative toward church as formerly. The other two are more negative about what church is today than they were five years ago; but they also have a concept of what church ought to be.

> *Dianne* They are trying to change people and it's not their job . . . . Church needs to be filled with people who need Jesus no matter what they look like or where they're at.

Church and Leadership

> *Helen*   Church is full of strange misfits, power hungry leaders and lots of ordinary bored people like me . . . . Less Sunday church + selfless Christianity applied Mon-Saturday would grow the real church.

Of the eight Alternative Faith Explorers, only one had any connection with a local church. The remaining seven seem uninvolved to the point of being quite uninterested. Several are tolerant of church but see it as completely irrelevant. It may help some, or be useful to some, or even be an "important social institution", but they see no value in it for themselves.

The Wayfinders interpret the question about church in a variety of ways. A number are highly critical of the institutional church. They see it as "largely irrelevant, tired and outdated, has lost its purpose, is in trouble". Some take care to distinguish the visible and the invisible church. While critical of the institutional church, many are positive about faith groups. Some do not identify these groups as 'church', others do describe the faith groups they are part of as 'church'.

Eleven Wayfinders are involved in some sort of faith group (although some comment that it's a group that doesn't worship, have communion or the Bible but is simply for discussion). Two Wayfinders have rare involvement with a church, attending less than once a month. Four have no current involvement in a church or faith group (one recently stopped attending a faith group but did not give a reason for doing so).

Some Wayfinders had fairly negative perspectives of church:

> *Melanie* I feel sad for that tired, outdated institution . . . . When I go on odd occasions I feel so glad to be 'out'. The group [I belong to] meets my need for worship, challenge, fun, deep relationships, family involvement.

> *Nigel*   I think it [church] is in trouble because of its inability to be accountable, open, and cater for mature, questioning Christians. I'm quite angry at pastors who seem to be more interested in retaining their own power . . . [but] I'm less angry with large churches these days because I've had active involvement in a smaller church.

66

Some on the other hand were positive, but with reservations:

Nicola [The church is] Precious to God, "the Bride". But – hard to come to terms with in practice, but still a source of strength/encouragement/ providing worship services.

Geoff I am optimistic that churches will grow to maturity . . . I personally relate to a wide variety of churches from Christian Gay stream down to pretty fundamentalist fellowships. I try to focus on the positives of each congregation.

Denis The church is a fragmentary representation of the life of the kingdom of God. Just as broken and frail as any other societal institution.

Wayfinders are clear about what they value and distrust when it comes to church.

- They value groups with rotational or highly participatory leadership.
- Many say they are happy to belong to a small-sized group.
- They value honesty, acceptance, challenge, and low expectations.
- They dislike what has come to be meaningless for them. "Can't face singing all those choruses ad infinitum/listening to the same old stories or sermons. I think I'm jaded."

LEADERSHIP

There is more agreement across all the groups about leadership than on any other question. Openness and humility are two qualities named by representatives of every group. Interestingly there is little mention of the content of belief or theology of Christian leaders, and even less mention of their personal relationship with God (perhaps this is taken for granted?).

The Returnees and Displaced emphasise:

- honesty
- integrity
- pure motives

- being 'real'
- an interest in people
- an attitude of servanthood
- adherence to biblical principles
- being led by God's Spirit, not by their own ambition
- accountability
- good people skills.

To this list the Exiles add:

- being real
- an educated understanding of co-dependency
- not having all the answers
- charisma, enthusiasm and vision.

Explorers commented more on what leaders should not be:

- not being a one man band
- not pursuing personal agendas
- not assuming they have exclusive truth
- not there to do the changing
- be a facilitator of the whole group
- expect to serve and be served.

The Alternative Faith Explorers spoke of the need for:

- training
- mutuality
- Christ-likeness
- being in touch with secular reality
- not having an 'us and them' mentality.

The Wayfinders wrote of the need for leaders who:

- are spiritually and psychologically mature
- are open to questions
- are able to listen well
- show empathy and understanding
- possess good people skills
- demonstrate a servant attitude.

More than any other groups the Wayfinders emphasised the need for:

- theological training
- strong pastoral training
- belief and acceptance of the Scriptures
- personal faith/contact with God
- being curious, searching and risk-taking
- providing direction and help for people's faith journeys
- being able to open up issues for people
- being willing to show weakness and fallibility and an understanding of their own shadow side
- living out of woundedness.

The following quotes express the hope of the Wayfinders regarding church leadership:

Jared   Honesty, integrity, openness, experience, ability to listen and a desire to relate deeply and meaningfully, and of course someone in contact with God.

Denis   Leadership would ideally open the issues of faith, biblical interpretation, personal, social and world issues and faith journeying and growth in the midst of these.

Three rejected the idea of individual leaders and describe their experience of group leadership which expects individual initiative and responsibility and values the wisdom and consensus of the group.

For those involved in church or faith group leadership, the preceding comments provide significant insights into the types of leadership tolerated, maybe even appreciated, by those outside the church.

8 The Role of Faith Groups

(Alan and Jenny)

IN THE ORIGINAL RESEARCH I (Alan) suggested that belonging to a faith group was highly influential in an individual's walk of faith. At that time however I did not have evidence to support this intuition.

This subsequent study, which shows how people have moved in their faith over a five year period, does now clearly indicate a relationship between faith group involvement and people making moves towards a clearer, personally stronger and more definitive Christian faith.

A Churchless Faith states "It appears that those who do *not* meet with others in the process of leaving or after leaving are less likely to move on from their faith position at the time of leaving the church." (p166) The Exiles and the Explorers are the groups most likely to have a fluid faith stance after leaving church. What happened to people in these groups?

EXILES

Eleven people who had originally been grouped among the Exiles returned questionnaires. Four of them remained in the same faith category five years on – that is, they were still Exiles. None of these four were part of any group or church; and neither were the three Exiles who moved to an alternative faith position. On the other hand, two of the three who moved to a Wayfarer faith stance were part of faith groups for a substantial time. In these faith groups they could discuss with others at similar stages their questions, concerns and experiences of

God and Christian faith. A connection between group involvement and subsequent faith development is indicated.

EXPLORERS

Seven people who were originally classified as Explorers responded to the questionnaire five years on. Here too, their movements over the five-year period demonstrate the influence that involvement in a group has on people's faith progression.

Three people had been part of faith groups. Two of these people were found to have moved to a faith position best described as Wayfinders. The third remained an Explorer.

Two other former Explorers had become part of Pentecostal churches again and their faith stance was now influenced by this involvement.

The two remaining original Explorers were not part of a faith group or church. One had a spiritual director and was still best described as Explorer. The other person had gone through a major faith and life change. This change was closely linked to a geographical shift which took him a long way from any Christian influence and immersed him in a different culture and lifestyle. This has had a strong effect on his faith and he would now be best described as an Exile. This situation will be discussed more fully below.

THE PLACE OF GROUPS

Clearly this study shows the significant influence of faith groups in people's individual faith journeys. With few exceptions, those people who have moved into a clearer, stronger and more definitive Christian faith have been participants in a faith group.

Of those who maintained a similar Explorer or Wayfinder faith position – a total of fourteen people – eleven had been part of faith groups. Of those who moved from an Exile or Explorer faith position in the direction of the Wayfinders – a total of five people – four had been part of a faith group. Altogether, fifteen of the nineteen people described either then or now as Explorers or Wayfinders have been participants in a faith group. This indicates that much can be gained by understanding the role and function of these groups.

Conversely, three Exiles moved in their faith understandings over the five-year period away from a distinctly Christian faith to an alternative faith position. None of these three were involved in a faith group. Jenny, Kevin and Heather describe their experience:

> *Heather* I don't [pray] in any sense that involves 'the other'. I don't hold any certain belief in this area [about God]. If anything [my] thoughts are negative because of what I thought I believed in for 25 years . . . [I've] moved a lot further down the continuum of no faith. If anything faith in 'self' is more important.

> *Kevin* I wouldn't categorise myself as apostate either in terms of trying to figure the big picture out. More like back at square one with a higher demand relative to evidence . . . I'm pretty much willing to believe anything if it has substance. Haven't found any specific substance yet . . . . Don't pray. Don't want to pray. IF God exists, then he is much more a personal entity for individuals, than has been shown.

> *Jenny* [My faith is now] much broader and not linked to any particular doctrine or religious set of guidelines. A general belief in a 'Higher Power', or spiritual realm beyond the physical. [About God I have] good thoughts mostly – still occasional twinges of the 'revengeful God' at times but mostly positive and hopeful that God (whatever or whoever) is a kindly soul.

In his work on faith development, James Fowler talks of the power of *Religio-cultural Force Fields*. These force fields are made up of the interactions, groups and affiliations people have. Belonging to a faith group represents one such force field that can encourage and 'fund' an individual's personal faith development. Groups produce a faith force field that affects individuals' motivation and provides models to be observed and critically assimilated.

The Role of Faith Groups

How this works is well illustrated by the experience of Spirited Exchanges. The rest of this chapter is written by Jenny McIntosh who facilitates this initiative.

To DETERMINE THE INFLUENCE and role of a processing group like Spirited Exchanges, I tracked as much as I know of the paths of people who have come to the Spirited Exchanges groups over the past six years. There seems to be a clear indication that many who engaged with their faith at a Spirited Exchanges group moved forward on their spiritual journey.

The people who came represented all the groups described in these chapters:

- Displaced Followers – those who are hurt and/or angry with a specific church but whose faith has remained bold and largely unchanged.
- Reflective Exiles – those for whom faith has become uncertain and questioned – the wheels have come off and they are critical and somewhat hostile in their stance towards faith and the church.
- Transitional Explorers – those who are more prepared to engage with faith again and find aspects of their faith that they can hold on to or new ways to understand faith paradigms.
- Integrated Wayfinders – those who have largely completed the task of rebuilding faith in ways that bring life, new ways of expression and greater connection to all aspects of their lives.

The Displaced Followers who came struggled with the challenges that others were making to their certainties. They often found it difficult to allow others to explore faith in the ways they needed to and they rose to its defence. Sometimes this people in this Displaced group changed their perspective or emphases but they held their new position with the same certainty and dogmatism that they had held the old. Their views sometimes led to healthy debate, with both ends of the spectrum being presented, thus giving parameters for those finding their way.

Someone commented once that the extremes helped her to know what she believed. She couldn't hold to one end any longer but she couldn't quite go to the other extreme either and so was able to find her place somewhere in the middle. At other times, however, the very definite and boldly-stated position of the Displaced Follower led to frustration and occasionally shut down input from others. Hence the emergence of the new guideline[22] given at the beginning of an evening: *we let God defend God.*

Over time it has become clear that Spirited Exchanges was more helpful for those whose faith was undergoing changes – that is, negotiating the shift from Exiles to Explorers to Wayfinders. People on this path are often very vulnerable and raw and if they have any faith stance it is very tentative. Often they are confused, and most of what they have previously believed is now uncertain.

One young woman in this Reflective Exile stage wrote about her experience. She quoted a poem by Jenny Bornholdt and then went on to give her own words to it:

WEIGHING UP THE HEART

Always, there are our hearts
to consider.
They are most
precious to us.

The heart is a means
of description.
It will locate
the sentiment.
Speak up
small red thing.

The heart is
the deciding factor.
Wave your arms around
see the sky bloom.

The heart lives
as a steady witness
within the body.

We would hope
for a rigorous
sympathy.
For the heart to
remember
the reliable place
in which it dwelled.

Always refer back
to the heart.
It is where
the world
began.

Jenny Bornholdt[23]

This poem was the theme of my year when I left church three years ago. It seemed to me to encapsulate the journey I was trying to embark on; a journey of solitude, deconstruction, and honesty. Of learning to listen to my heart.

"Speak up, small red thing", I often said to myself as screeds of other voices, narratives, ideas, and 'shoulds' echoed around my head. I'd had enough of other people's ideas. Their ideas about God, the world, my place in the world, how to be a good person, how I could best serve and follow God . . . . It had got to the point where I no longer knew what I thought . . . . The way people at my church seemed to connect with God felt so different to me. People's prayers made no sense to me. As time went by, church services became more and more a negative experience. I would feel frustrated and more disillusioned . . . . Things felt empty and dark and hard.

This young woman attended a Spirited Exchanges group for about two years. She commented concerning the group: "The conversations we've had in this group are one of the things that have been really helpful for me in discovering a new faith. Little by little, I have felt comfortable saying that I believe in . . . a spirit of goodness that exists in the world . . . which might have something to do with our lives . . . a creator spirit . . . God (both female and male) . . . this God is so much bigger than we can comprehend . . . . This God loves people in the world . . . this God loves me . . . ."

Further on again she said: "Recently, it dawned on me that I think I trust God again. I couldn't pinpoint when I started to feel that, or even necessarily why, but I knew I did. And I want to follow and honour this God with my life."

This young woman's faith would once have been described as strong and definite, and much of her life was dedicated to church activities and to serving God. Then bit by bit her faith fell into disarray to a degree where all she had was "occasional glimpses of God in nature" and at that point she left the church. Initially she had many questions, doubts and conflicting ideas buzzing around in her head. Then, little by little, she was able to engage with faith again and find new ways of believing in God to the point where she became more confident about wanting to follow this God.

A man who attended a Spirited Exchanges group for a couple of years and had stopped believing in the God he had once been taught to believe in, came to the place of saying: "Spirituality and faith have become integral to me – as an expression of my self and who God is through me, rather than who God is in spite of me. Every day becomes more mysterious, more frustrating and at the same time, more comforting, loving and benevolent. It is in this duality that I can connect with the world around me."

Another woman, after she had been in the group for a considerable period, put it this way: "I still have many questions. But I have discovered something of the beauty of mystery, of things that are 'too wonderful for me, too lofty for me to attain'. I feel that my spiritual journey was one that required me to die on the inside in order to truly come alive to God, a God that was a lot bigger than I'd ever imagined."

And yet another woman said: "Somehow, I think more than ever, I believe in a God who above all else is utterly loving. And that provides a more compelling reason than anything else I can think of for pursuing a relationship with God in the face of doubt. I strongly believe that doubt is not indicative of a faith that is weak. Doubt is inevitable. It's human and it's honest. To have the freedom to voice that doubt without being judged is so important. To have the courage to explore the doubt, that is what gives faith its strength. Faith has to be dynamic, not static, because life grinds on and its experiences continually mould us. Our faith has to be able to incorporate what we experience of our world otherwise it is based on nothing that has any meaning for us."

By the Wayfinder stage people are stronger again in what they believe. They can sit with unanswered questions and with mystery. They have come to a place where faith has greater connection to their experiences and to the world in general. It is bigger, and able to encompass paradox.

By the Wayfinder stage also, people are moving on from Spirited Exchanges. They recognise that their faith has changed and is now different from that of the newer people coming into the group. They are ready to explore new patterns and practices of expressing their faith.

The movement out of Spirited Exchanges is an important one. What do people move on to? The pattern seems to be as follows:

- some move to a group of similar-minded people and develop a way of being a faith community together.
- some move to re-engagement in a church, usually a very different style from the one they came out of previously. They are likely to be less frequent in attendance and less dependent on the community of faith as a place of belonging socially. Their communities of belonging are broader.
- many find a spiritual director very helpful at this stage if they haven't already been seeing one.
- others remain detached from committing to a particular group and do something of a pick and mix to sustain their faith. A Taizé service here, communion there and a retreat somewhere else, or a mix of any of the above. The outdoors and nature feature for some.

Coming to the group over a period of time, usually months or years, enabled people to work through the stages from Exile to Explorer to Wayfinder, depending where on the continuum they were. Indeed, I would presume to say their attendance enhanced the process. That is not to say that Spirited Exchanges was the sole influence for these people, but it was a significant one. Other strong supports were one-to-one work with a spiritual director or someone else who understood the journey, books, retreats and different styles of worship services such as Celtic or Taizé. Spirited Exchanges and groups with a similar ethos seem to be a key catalyst for people to make the transition from one stage to another.

9 Conclusions from the Study

(Alan)

IN THIS CHAPTER WE WILL CONSIDER the conclusions from the research. For now we will focus on the core research convictions themselves without seeking to interpret them or suggest specific responses to them. In the chapters that follow we will reflect on responses to church leavers. These chapters will discuss in more detail the impact and implications of the research findings. Jenny will recount the story of the development of Spirited Exchanges and each of us will offer a chapter giving our individual perspectives as a pastor (Alan), a spiritual director (Adrienne), and a counsellor and facilitator of groups for church leavers (Jenny).

The conclusions fall into three major categories:

- conclusions about the validity of the faith categories developed in *A Churchless Faith*
- conclusions about people's connections with established forms of church
- conclusions specifically about the faith of the leavers.

RESEARCH AND THE FAITH CATEGORIES DEVELOPED

1. Five years on, the faith categories developed in *A Churchless Faith* continue to be useful as explanatory tools and as descriptors of the faith positions of church leavers. The six categories (Returnees, Displaced, Exiles, Explorers, Alternative Faith Explorers and Wayfinders) were used by the four people involved in this study to determine the faith position of each person based on their responses to the questionnaire.

The categories were easily interpreted and used by the four researchers, both independently and in subsequent discussions.

2. The original research predicted that the Exiles and Explorers were the most unstable faith positions and that people in these positions were likely to move away from these less stable positions towards the more grounded Wayfinder, Displaced or Alternative Faith positions. The findings of this Five Years On study support these predictions. The Exiles (64%) and Explorers (72%) exhibited the greatest faith change over the five year period.

3. The original research postulated that being part of a faith group was a powerful context, encouraging continued faith development. This was borne out in the findings of the Five Years On study. (See the chapter on the role of faith groups.)

4. There may be merit in contacting this group of church leavers in another five years to record and assess their continuing journey of faith. Longitudinal studies such as this provide valuable insights on people's faith trajectories.

CONNECTIONS WITH ESTABLISHED CHURCHES

1. Having left an EPC church people are unlikely to rejoin one. Only four people who had left an EPC church have gone back to regular participation in any form of established Christian church during the last five years.

This does not include the six people who returned questionnaires who had never left the church. Three of these were Wayfinders who had never left the church although they had created some internal distance from it while working through their own personal faith changes. Two of the three, a married couple, were involved in a small main-line traditional church in a marginalised ethnic community. This couple were not themselves part of this ethnic group but were part of the church because of their social-justice and mission convictions. The husband said of church – "I personally relate to a wide variety of churches, from the Christian Gay Stream right through to the pretty fundamentalist fellowships. I try to focus on the positives of each congregation . . . and do not think it appropriate to challenge the 'immature' or inconsistent aspects of congregational life, expectant that God in his own time will draw these issues to the attention of the congregations. Over the last five years, I would say that my tolerance for congregations at the edge of orthodoxy has grown, trusting that positives for God's kingdom will result."

The third person in this group said he attended a church on average once a month – "I just attend with no other commitment. My faith life is lived in my daily experience. The Sunday church expression of this is a minimal part of my experience."

These quotes indicate the type and role of established churches in the faith of Wayfinders. The remaining 14 Wayfinders had no regular connection to an established form of church. Many, however, were actively involved in faith groups. These faith groups were not connected to any established church.

The remaining three of the six who had not left the church were originally interviewed because they were on the edge of leaving. Five years later we see that in fact they never actually left the EPC church. One remained part of the church he had been at for a number of years. The other two moved from one EPC church to another.

Taken together these results indicate:

- Having left, very few people will return to regular involvement in any form of established church within five years.
- Many who are apparently on the edge of leaving an EPC church may in fact not leave.
- Few Wayfinders having left church go on to reconnect with established forms of church. Those who do (3 out of 17) had consistently retained connections with an established church.

2. There was a consistent concern about church. ALL the respondents expressed reservations, significant concerns or clear antipathy to established churches. For most, church was simply irrelevant to their faith and life. Considering the deep and long term commitment these

people had previously made to their churches (on average being adult committed members for 15.8 years) this must raise serious concerns for those responsible for shaping churches today.

3. People across all faith categories raised significant concerns with regard to leadership in faith and church groups. Universally, the leavers looked primarily for 'character' strengths including integrity, vulnerability, and willingness to express weakness. The Wayfinders especially pointed to the need for theological and pastoral training, spiritual and psychological maturity and the deep personal skills of empathy and listening.

The universal concerns and specific advice of the Wayfinders raise significant questions regarding the priorities of church leaders and leader training.

THE FAITH OF THE LEAVERS

1. Over the five year period the majority of respondents showed stability in their faith position. Most did not move faith category in the five year period. This was particularly the case for:
- The Displaced and Returnees – 68% no change
- Alternative Faith Explorers – 100% no change
- Wayfinders – 90% no change.

The two faith categories where there was substantial movement were the Exiles (36% no change – 64% movement) and Explorers (28% no change – 72% movement).

Across all the faith categories 68% (n=32) remained in the same faith position five years on.

The stability of these faith positions across the five-year period challenges prevailing views about the faith of church leavers. Many, perhaps especially those in church leadership, would draw a connection between leaving church and a loss of faith. The results of this study would not support this view.

The faith stability of the Wayfinders (90%) across the five year period while most (77%) have no connection to any form of church raises questions for church leaders who see their own structures as essential to an ongoing maturing of Christian faith.

2. Whether they are discussion groups or groups that take on elements of church worship, faith groups for teaching and support beyond the established church are powerful contexts for continued individual faith development. Of the nineteen people described as Explorers or Wayfinders, including those who remained stable in these positions across the five years and those who moved into them, fifteen (79%) were part of faith groups.

As Professor James Fowler suggests, being part of such a group provides a faith force field that encourages and supports personal faith development.

3. The differing faith categories reflect responsiveness to differing types and ways of prayer, rituals, use of symbols and differing approaches to the Bible. Understanding and being able to draw on a variety of approaches may enable faith groups and churches to be relevant to the faith needs of a variety of Christian people.

4. The faith described by the Wayfinders, in particular, is compelling in at least two significant areas:

- *Theological* The Wayfinders describe their faith in specifically orthodox Christian ways. The accounts they give of their faith express strong continuities with evangelical expressions of faith. The faith descriptions of the Wayfinders do not reflect a move to liberalism, agnosticism, 'new age' spirituality, or humanism.
- *Cultural* The dynamic, open, organic, constantly developing faith described by the Wayfinders with its intimate connections to the totality of their lives appears culturally attractive.

SUMMARY

In this chapter we have considered some key conclusions drawn from the questionnaires of the respondents five years after first being interviewed. The ability to compare and contrast each individual's faith development across a five-year period is unique in studies of church leavers. Therefore the conclusions suggest new glimpses in an area where anecdotal evidence and hunches have previously dominated.

RESPONDING TO CHURCH LEAVERS

10 The Development of Spirited Exchanges

(Jenny)

THE FINDINGS OF THE FIRST STUDY (outlined in Chapter 1) began to become available to the public in 1998 in the form of articles and presentations to groups. People for whom this research resonated became very interested and keen to explore it further. This research affirmed and validated the faith journeys of a large number of people who had either left the established church or were struggling to remain there. It provided a framework that enabled people to better understand the dynamics at play in their changing faith paradigms. It also gave a new vocabulary for people to now be able to name what was happening within them.

I was one of those for whom these findings were a lifeline. I was experiencing a faith crisis and confusion and I had no words, and no safe people with whom to talk through my inner turmoil – only a strong sense that I was dying spiritually and no longer felt like I fitted in the church.

An article published in *Canvas* magazine early in 1997 was my first introduction to Alan and the research he was doing. Prior to reading this article called *Should I stay or should I go?*[24] I had wondered if I was losing my faith. The article, which included a brief summary of Fowler's stages of faith, gave a very different slant to anything I had been taught and was very timely for me. It named and validated what I was experiencing and gave me a sense of hope for the future. It offered me a way forward. Might it even be that God was beckoning me?

I think it also gave me the realisation that what was happening to me was not something that I had caused or was my fault. I hadn't gone out looking for it. Nor was it something to which I could apply an easy formula and all would be well again. Alan's article was indicating that there could be a pull to go further, away from the known pathways, and that was OK. It meant that I had to set out on this journey myself and find where those new pathways might lead.

I began with a six-month trial period of leaving the church I had been a part of for 19 years. In that time I either didn't attend church or tried out other churches. My feeling of not fitting only grew. The leaving was painful and something I didn't do thoughtlessly. I was leaving a group of people I cared about, many of whom were close friends. They had supported my family while we worked overseas for a number of years and stood by me after the sudden death of my husband, also their minister at the time. My children were still a part of it. It was my local church and had been an integral part of my life – in many ways, leaving it felt something similar to what a divorce must feel like. And yet it was something I knew I had to do if I was going to find life in my faith again. Having made the move I didn't go back. At the end of the six months I went to one service to bring closure to the time I had been involved there and to honour the people who had been a part of that. I was keen to leave well and remain in relationship with those still there. It was important to me that I could meet them in my local supermarket and not feel awkward bumping into them.

Then for a year or so I sat on the edges of a church that was able to encompass diversity of faith expression and outlook. Just after I arrived, Alan was appointed as minister to the church. At the end of that year a new chapter began as my experiences of struggling with church and faith, my training as a counsellor, and my availability for a new job coincided with Alan's thinking about possible practical ways to respond to people he was encountering as a result of the publication of his thesis. Thus began the germination of Spirited Exchanges at the beginning of 1999.

Spirited Exchanges was the name we gave initially to a Sunday evening open discussion forum. 'Spirited' described the kind of discussion we hoped it would be as people shared their thinking and experiences with one another; and also acknowledged the Holy Spirit as a very integral part of what was going on. 'Exchanges' indicated that this was an interactive and conversational exchange of opinions and discussion rather than one person speaking from the front telling us how or what we should believe. This is quite a different paradigm to usual church meetings. The validity of these elements still holds today, seven years later, where Spirited Exchanges is the umbrella term for a number of different initiatives which offer support, accompaniment and resources for those in faith stage transition, many who have left the institutional church.

The original group met on a Sunday evening, beginning at 6.30 p.m. It was held in the basement of Wellington Central Baptist Church.[25] Here is how someone described her first experience of attending a Spirited Exchanges gathering.

> I arrived at the church and followed the arrows marked 'Spirited Exchanges' downstairs to a large basement room which was set up at one end in semi café style. A number of round tables with chairs were set in a rough circle. The room was dimly lit with candles on the tables and there was some music, I can't remember what, playing in the background. As I and others arrived, we were invited to help ourselves to homemade cake and freshly brewed coffee. Some books and reprints of articles were spread on a separate table toward the back. A couple of people were browsing through those.

Approximately fifteen minutes later, Jenny invited people to take their seats and begin the discussion. She started by welcoming us and introducing us to the whys and whats of Spirited Exchanges. The key point was that this is an open-ended discussion forum for people who are struggling with faith and church issues. In this place we could try out our thinking, raise our questions and doubts. It was OK to say anything. Nothing was considered heretical. We could even change our minds during the course of the evening if we wanted to. Use this space and time in ways that are helpful for you – that was the message.

There were some guidelines designed to keep the space 'safe' for everyone. The main thing to remember was that this was a conversation, not a monologue. No one was a guru; each person's opinion was equally worthy of respect.

The guidelines were also listed on a piece of paper on the resource table and were as follows:

- we are not trying to produce one answer that everyone must adhere to
- there is freedom for differing views and opinions and we ask for respect for those no matter how different or heretical these might sound
- we ask for respect and space for each person who comes and for their opinions
- we cannot 'fix it' for people who come
- because this is a conversation we ask that each person speaks relatively briefly
- we have no neat 'tie-up' at the end
- we let God defend God.

Somebody referred to this introduction as the 'fasten your seat belt' spiel so I gathered it was a regular preamble to the evening.

After this a guy told something of his faith journey to the rest of the group. Clearly this had been set up beforehand. He seemed quite at ease in the group so I assumed he had been coming for a while. It was quite special, being able to hear about someone else's life and faith struggles and experiences. It felt like you had been taken into someone's inner world and what a privilege that was. It was also quite comforting to realise that in a number of ways my journey was similar to his. We were asked to respect the confidentiality of his story and he was gracious enough to allow us to ask questions if we wanted to.

Jenny then introduced the discussion topic which for this evening was 'Is there a plan or is life a random series of events?' There was a strip of tape down the length of the room and we were each given a sticker to mark the spot where we would locate ourselves on a continuum between the two poles of that statement. We then discussed the topic at our tables. This felt more comfortable than talking in the bigger group would have been. Some people chose to just listen and not say much. One man remained anonymous and virtually silent throughout the evening and that seemed to be acceptable.

The discussion was at times robust and at other times more reflective. There was quite a long silence at one stage which no one leapt to fill. While it got a bit uncomfortable it was good too as it enabled people to process what was being said. A few times it got a bit 'heady' and at one point Jenny made us aware of that and suggested that we talk more out of our experience rather than theoretically. But she largely just let the conversation run, with only one or two questions thrown in. She seemed to play a role of lightly facilitating but also became one of the participants of the discussion sharing the same struggles as the rest of the group.

After about an hour and a half Jenny brought the conversation to an end at a natural juncture. Some people left, others stayed and continued the conversation informally.

My own further observations/comments:

It was neither a therapy session nor an intellectual debate although at times veered towards the latter.

Being in a church basement was not a neutral space, but it did have the benefit of being private – unlike a café or a pub. The café style atmosphere and the dim light gave a comfortable feeling of anonymity.

The group felt like a safe place to explore quite sensitive and even painful issues. It was a non-judgmental environment where it was OK to put out your opinions, even if they were only half-formed. People were able to be real, they could swear if they wanted to and there were no shocked or furtive looks their way. The way it operated did measure up to the guidelines read out. I felt like I could say what I wanted to and that was OK, that I was respected and also that I was being treated as an 'adult'. Hard to believe but there genuinely seemed to be no agenda that people would have to go back to church again after this process was over.

I was stimulated by the experience and think I will venture back in a fortnight when it meets again.

As the group was forming we held regular times to evaluate how it was going with the group. Their feedback about what they found helpful and how we should proceed helped us to learn better what people needed and how we could best respond. One very gratifying comment from a person who attended regularly was that the power in the group was nowhere and everywhere. That was the dynamic we had hoped to establish. We wanted to communicate our assumption that people were adults taking charge of their own faith journey. We were not looking to make decisions for them.

One of the most crucial characteristics of these groups is safety. People need to know that:

- There is no expectation or agenda that people will return to church or are expected to follow any particular way of thinking or believing.

- They can say anything and not have it shut down by others.
- Their opinions will be respected. Often leavers are mistrustful of other Christians who, they feel, will be trying to get them to fit the box again. This experience needs to be reversed. People need to be able to say what is real for them at the time, however heretical or unmentionable in a church setting. For example: "I just don't know if I believe in any of this stuff any more" or "I'm not sure I'd even call myself a Christian now". This can be necessary for some to move forward on the journey.
- There can be anonymity if required and confidentiality within the group.
- There is no pressure on them to tell more of their story than they want to or are ready to.

Hence such a group needs a facilitator who is mindful of and in control of these factors; and it needs established guidelines agreed to by those present.

M Scott Peck in his book *The Different Drum* describes such a space as "a safe place precisely because no one is attempting to heal or convert you, to fix you, to change you. Instead the members accept you as you are. You are free to be you. And being so free, you are free to discard defences, masks, disguises; free to seek your own psychological and spiritual health; free to become your whole and holy self."[26]

People have said of Spirited Exchanges:

"I can be me."

"I can say what I like and not be rubbished or written off."

"People want to hear what I have to say."

"I can be quiet, and no-one will pester me or ask that I contribute."

"I can ask questions that I would hesitate to ask in a church gathering."

"I can feel safe and accepted."

"I can find some handles for my current situation."

"I find others in a similar place and can hear voiced something of my own journey."

"I can try out my new thoughts on others and hear what they sound like without being held to them forevermore."

Seven years down the track, Spirited Exchanges is the umbrella name for a variety of initiatives that have been developed to offer support, help resource and accompany those on a faith journey outside of the church.

In addition to the safe and open ended discussion forums described above Spirited Exchanges includes:

A newsletter Initially published bimonthly it is now put out ten times a year. It contains people's stories of their struggles with church or with faith; articles about topics of interest (such as stages of faith, spiritual abuse, faith and mental health); poetry; book reviews and a space for readers to respond.

Resources Guidelines and suggestions for facilitating groups for church leavers; a library of helpful books and articles; a manual on stages of faith development; connections with other individuals and groups sharing similar concerns.

Listening Within the groups and one to one; face to face, by telephone or by e-mail.

Training Seminars and workshops to help people within churches and in wider Christian circles understand what occurs for people who leave church and the whole concept of faith stage transition. Also training for potential facilitators of groups.

A website www.spiritedexchanges.org.nz makes the newsletters and other information available online.

International connections A group of people in the UK are in the process of developing a network there based on the principles and patterns of Spirited Exchanges.

What began as something of an experiment is now an established and proven resource for people in faith stage transition.

11 A Spirited Exchanges Perspective on the Research

(Jenny)

> "How can I know what I mean until I hear what I say?"
> (Harriet Beecher Stowe in *Uncle Tom's Cabin*)

> "Be who you are and say what you feel because those who
> mind don't matter and those who matter don't mind."
> (Dr. Seuss)

WHAT STRIKES ME FROM THIS RESEARCH is the importance of a place, like Spirited Exchanges or some other similar group, for people in transition between faith stages. It seems vital that people have a place which provides support and gives understanding and safety to them while they process the issues that have come up for them: that they can ask the questions, explore the doubts of faith and try out new ways of believing in an environment that is open and non-judgemental.

Maree, interviewed in *A Churchless Faith*, says:

> You have got to have that sounding board, you have got to talk with people. I think it's their experiences that shed light on my own. I've got a couple of friends who I would call quite good thinkers, people who are searching out things, and getting their feedback has been tremendously invaluable. In a way, even though you find things being stripped away, you also find that foundation of faith there.

For those who are struggling with doubts and questions about faith and church and are traversing that uncultivated land between faith stages (Exile to Explorer to Wayfinder), that 'sounding board' or group is an important part of the process. Such a group serves a number of functions:

Validation and normalisation of the journey Meeting others experiencing similar changes to their faith is enormously encouraging and helps them to understand that this could be OK. There are other people for whom this is happening as well.

Supportive companionship, others to journey with This is hugely important as previous supports would have most likely been in the church and are now usually no longer available. It is a very lonely and isolated position to be in.

Education The group has an educative function. It provides understanding of the 'wilderness' or 'desert' place in the faith journey and points to resources that might help people chart this less known territory. It raises awareness of faith as a journey and introduces the concept of faith stage development

Guiding voices People sharing their experiences of the journey can point to the next foothold for others who come. Because a group includes people at various stages on the journey those further along are modelling the next stages for those starting out. For example, people living comfortably with paradox and open-endedness will be talking about the way they now express their faith. This may resonate for someone else as an idea to pursue. The guiding voices may also be in books – the journeys of other pilgrims, both contemporary and from the past.

Being a 'sounding board' As people voice their doubts and questions others are there to hear them, reflect back and engage with the issues and ideas that have been raised. When others interact with them and nod or shake their heads, the ideas and uncertainties which have previously only gone round and round in their heads become more formed and concrete. Further down the track as the explorer gains more confidence and tentatively tries out new paradigms of faith belief and expression, it is important for them to hear themselves speaking out what they believe – "how can I know what I mean until I hear what I say?" At Spirited Exchanges we say that it is OK for people to change their minds from one week to another or even within the same evening if they want to. Often people don't know how something is going to sound until they say it aloud it in front of others and in so hearing they decide to own it or dismiss it. It is about trying out new understandings with the rest of the group and seeing how they sit. In this way people form new ways of seeing and believing, which are lifegiving and have integrity for them.

Also sometimes the act of owning things and saying them out loud, particularly negative or blaming things, brings a freedom, a release that enables the person to let them go and so move on in the journey. When people can't let things go progress is stymied.

Motivation Knowing there is a regular group meeting offers the opportunity for people to engage with others when the time seems right for them to do so. When people leave churches they sometimes want to put a lot of distance between them and anything to do with church. That can lead to letting the concerns drift, leaving many of the issues unresolved, and maybe letting faith slip altogether, rather than making a decision one way or the other. Knowing there is a group which facilitates some of the process of engaging with the issues means they don't start with a blank page and have to do it all themselves. There are others who know and understand and have an interest in the wellbeing of those who leave.

People participating in this kind of group are allowed to say and think what they want to and to direct their own faith paths. They increasingly determine what they feel they need to develop their faith rather than hand that responsibility over to the institutional church to direct and shape. There is a growing independence of thinking that develops as people gain confidence in exploring and expressing what they might believe.

Being part of this sort of group enables people to find their voice and develop the confidence to try it out. This is a big thing for people who have been taught to obey the rules and believe the prescriptions of faith from their leaders and others around no matter what. It is even more significant for those who have been severely chastised for deviating from pre-packaged faith or questioning the party line. For people from that kind of background it can take some time to shift the feelings of accompanying guilt and be able to stand more firmly with their internal voice.

Sometimes it is more subtle than that. They may not openly rebuke, but many leaders quite strongly prescribe the parameters of belief and give a clear message that to disagree would be wrong. This doesn't allow people to develop their own internal strength of faith. In working with church leavers I have encountered numerous people who have related stories of being told they hadn't enough faith or they can't be Christians or believers if they believe such and such or dare to question what they have been taught.

Sometimes I would describe the control and restrictions by church leaders and culture as spiritual abuse. "Spiritual Abuse can occur when a leader uses his or her *spiritual position* to control or dominate another person. It often involves overriding the feelings and opinions of another, without regard to what will result in the other person's state of living, emotions or spiritual well-being. In this application power is used to bolster the position or needs of a leader, over and above the one who comes to them in need . . . . Spiritual abuse can also occur when *spirituality* is used to make others live up to a 'spiritual standard'. This promotes external 'spiritual performance' also without regard to an individual's actual well-being, or is used as a means of 'proving' an individual's spirituality . . . ."[27]

Whatever the case, the results of spiritual abuse are usually the same: the individual is left bearing the weight of guilt, judgment or condemnation, and confusion about their worth and standing as a Christian.

This is a complex issue with numerous strands that need unravelling. For the purposes of this book I would just like to say that depending on the degree of spiritual abuse a person has encountered, there may be need for some one-to-one interaction with a counsellor or spiritual director before moving to the group or alongside being part of a group. Depression is a common outcome for people who have been subject to spiritual abuse and it takes some time for them to find their own voice and thus feel empowered. When they do, they need a group of understanding people to support them while they develop confidence in themselves.

The findings from the Five Years On study reinforce the need for groups like Spirited Exchanges. Being part of a group definitely facilitates the movement between the stages – Exile to Explorer to Wayfinder. Unfortunately at this stage in church history it is difficult to make these transitions while staying within the institutional church. When people are with others on something of the same journey, in this context, they have freedom to express the doubts, ask the questions and bat around the dilemmas confronting them without the risk of destabilising someone else's faith or feeling they are being judged.

Groups improve the chances of people staying on the faith journey because they have a yardstick to go by. They see and hear of the experiences and new discoveries of others in similar space, others who have been where they are on the journey. Rachel, an Exile quoted in Chapter Two, who five years on is still an Exile, says "I don't know where I am faith-wise as I have no-one to compare myself with – and I don't know if there is a measurement." She says she no longer fits in the church. If she had been able to be part of a group she may have had the incentive and encouragement to do the processing and searching for new ways of faith belief and expression.

For Rachel, being in the Reflective Exile faith zone makes for struggle and despair. It is lonely, misunderstood, confusing and painful. Some of that is necessary to propel a person to search for new meaning and understanding of God, but it can also leave them floundering as to what to do next. There is often no community around to support them through this, nor do they have the security of a sure faith to fall back on when things get rough. While there is a degree of relief in being free of what felt like constraint and boxed-in faith, there is also insecurity. It is clear that Rachel does not have a settled faith stance. She can neither give it up completely nor feel any confidence in what she believes.

A person who is able to make the transition through to the Integrated Wayfinder stage finds faith has new life again. There is an internal strengthening, a willingness to go with their inner authority. They will express their faith differently from how they did previously. Worship, prayer, their approach to the Bible will all be different. They will experience it as much more holistic, much more integrated into all of life. Their faith and experiences of life and the world now have much more congruity. Rob spoke of it this way in *A Churchless Faith*:

> I see so many Christians talk about worshipping God but they are oblivious to the fact that they are ecologically a cancer on the planet ... I say you can't worship God on a Sunday morning and desecrate this planet all through the week ....[28]

He regards his reading in the area of ecology as "food for the soul".

Such integrated faith is usually broader. People are often more open to understanding and even drawing from people of other religions. They have a more open stance towards thorny issues such as abortion and homosexuality. The Integrated Wayfinder is the best outcome for those who want to stay on the journey. They don't have to have neat answers to everything and they sit comfortably with the open-endedness of that.

Rebecca, who came through a Spirited Exchanges group, described it this way:

> My faith is now broader and deeper and more honest than before. I no longer feel I have to pretend that Christianity

holds the answers to everything. I'm OK that it doesn't. God is and I am. I believe God is in and around and under and over me and somehow works in that mix and companions me, but I don't believe that God is as interventionist as I once did. I have incorporated new images of God that are more life-giving. My faith is deeper and more integrated into all of who I am. This has been so freeing and enables me to be more myself, which in turn is the task I believe we are called to – to realise our unique potential and live into that.

If people are not able to express and explore their questions and doubts, several things can happen. The first is that they stay in the same place, like Rachel, not finding anything life-giving in faith any more. In some ways they are not freed to believe and not freed to live without belief. Secondly, they can push the questions away and stick with the status quo, with the result that they will never really grow further. In this option they are denying both their own inner voice and a significant life stage transition catalyst.[29] They will always remain in a place of receiving their faith from outside, from what others tell them and give them and deem acceptable, even if for them it doesn't fit. And thirdly, I believe it is a denying of the call of God and the call of self to a deeper and more truthful and balanced place, and that perhaps is the most significant point of all.

Churches and church leaders want to protect people's faith. With this good motive they have sometimes circumscribed or even shut down natural and God-given transition processes. Such processes lead to a more expansive, sustaining and lively faith, yet churches often seem to fear to allow people to engage with the questions, doubts and struggles which are a natural part of transition. If instead we trust and affirm the processes we allow the Holy Spirit to move and create in us radical new ways of being and living our faith. Spirited Exchanges groups have a significant role in affirming these processes and offering support and hope to people on this journey.

12 How can a Spiritual Director help?

(Adrienne)

WHEN ALAN OFFERED ME THE OPPORTUNITY to analyse the responses to the questionnaires for this study I assumed at first it would be a fairly academic exercise. I was very interested in the research because I had my own struggles with faith. I had participated in Spirited Exchanges meetings on a fairly regular basis and discovered by experience and observation how helpful this kind of group could be. But I didn't anticipate how very relevant this research would be to my work as a spiritual director.[30]

As I began analysing the questionnaires for this study I felt I had been given a gold mine. The raw material here is invaluable and perhaps unique. Many books have been written by theologians and pastors concerning the experience of faith. But in this study we have access to the thoughts and experience of ordinary people at different stages of faith, writing in their own words their reflections on prayer, on their beliefs, on maturity, on their encounters with God.

While this material is helpful and thought provoking in a general sense, in this chapter I am focusing in particular on its implications for spiritual direction with church leavers, and those who have issues with church, or with Christian faith, or with both.

What impressed me most forcefully in this material was the comparison between the responses of the Displaced and Returnees on the one hand and the Wayfinders on the other. People in all these groups generally affirmed a strong faith, made a practice of prayer and had a sense of growing in their relationship with God. However their language in responding to the questions of the survey is quite diverse. The Displaced and the Returnees tended to use conventional words and phrases to describe their faith and their experiences of God and prayer. The Wayfinders by contrast used a much wider range of vocabulary.

In saying this I'm not judging the reality of the faith or the depth of the experience of people in any group but simply observing that the language they use reflects their stage of faith. It shows the difference between the 'received faith', largely unexamined and simply accepted, and the 'integrated faith' of the Wayfinders which has been examined, tested, and shaped to become the individual's own.

A number of the Wayfinders mention having experience of spiritual direction. But nearly all in this group, it seems to me, whether they are in formal spiritual direction or not, show evidence of the sort of reflection and connection that is fostered and flourishes in a healthy spiritual direction relationship.

The fact that this study concerned people from EPC churches has some significance. Spiritual direction has not generally been part of these traditions. This would be one reason why we might see few of the Displaced approaching a Spiritual Director. Spiritual direction is gaining a higher profile in EPC circles however and as this happens we may get more people who are disaffected with church looking for it. Some of them may be seeking a form of pastoral care no longer available to them in their churches. Some may be wounded, angry, disillusioned or simply tired. They need a safe place to talk these issues through. It has been my experience that for some such people a few sessions are enough to restore their sense of balance and they may then withdraw from the relationship. These people undoubtedly have problems with church, but they are not asking the 'meta-questions' at this stage. Others however may find they are beginning a new stage in their spiritual journey. They are ready to begin the work of examining and reflecting on their faith.

Laura is an example of a person in the Displaced group who is perhaps ready to start such a walk. She writes from within the context of recent bereavement and her language reveals the split between her belief ("I know he is treating me gently") and her experience ("I am feeling wounded by the Lord"). Whether or to what extent Laura may have reflected on this gulf between head knowledge and heart experience is impossible to say. But noticing and lovingly attending to such moments of truth is the stuff of spiritual direction. As ever, the spiritual director has to find the delicate balance between supporting people in the place where they now are and helping them to discern the moment when they are ready to move on.

The other groups in this study are those who clearly are now dealing with the meta-questions. Some of these withdraw from all faith connections and would therefore not be interested in spiritual direction. Others, while reacting against their own churches, might still desire some sort of Christian spiritual connection. Perhaps the Exiles are wary – but the Explorers may be ready to try something new.

There is one large group of people which is not specifically covered in this study but to which many of its discoveries apply. These are the people described as 'internal leavers'.[31] For whatever reason, they cannot or do not choose to leave their church. They may be married to the pastor. They may wish to stay for the sake of their children. They may be in some sort of Christian employment that requires church attendance. Highly critical Displaced, lonely Exiles, tentative Explorers, privately disbelieving Alternative Faith people may well be hidden in almost every church congregation.

Whether they've left the church, or remain unobserved and unhappy within it, or simply have a desire to explore and grow, for people wanting to pursue their journey of faith spiritual direction may be a lifeline. What can it offer? A group of Wellington Spiritual Directors came up with the following ideas:

> *Opportunity to tell the story* The sort of pastoral listening Alan describes in the following chapter is equally fundamental to spiritual direction.

Honouring the place where they are The spiritual director has no agenda to get people back into a church or to sort out their spiritual problems for them. (In this he or she differs from even the most sympathetic pastor.)

Permission to explore For me this is one of the most joyful aspects of my work as a spiritual director. For instance, I listen to people who are bruised by their perceived failure to pray 'properly'. I hear the anxiety of those who have begun to question what they previously believed implicitly. I have the delight of helping them to discover that there are multiple ways to pray; and that questions and doubts can be entertained, not banished.

Validation – affirmation For people emerging from or struggling with authoritarian structures this is crucial. Many EPC churches have a very strong leadership style, very clear-cut rules and guidelines for living, a very definite theological stance. A few can only be described as abusive in their expectation or insistence that everyone conforms. In contrast, the respectful, non-judgmental listening of a Spiritual Director can give the sense that it is OK to trust one's own 'knowing'. People can grow in confidence that they have the ability and the right to evaluate what is said and done and expected in church; and to make their own decisions and responses.

Creating community Loneliness can be a huge issue for people who have left church. They may feel misunderstood, blamed, a pariah to former friends. A spiritual director not only offers the gift of accompaniment but may be able to point them to events or groups where they can interact with others walking a similar path. Reassurance that they are not alone in their struggles is part of this.

New 'languages of faith', new images of God As people explore different aspects of faith they may well find they need a new vocabulary to describe what is happening to them. Words and phrases associated with previous church connections may now seem irrelevant or clichéd. This is certainly highlighted in the study, with many Wayfinders deliberately choosing to use words outside the common jargon of EPC culture to talk about their present faith. Spiritual direction is an opportunity to play with new words and new ideas. Damaging, abusive images of God can be discarded and life-giving, liberating ones can be embraced. Of course, some people can and do make this transition without help, but many value the support and 'permission' of a spiritual director.

Resources for personal growth In addition to accompaniment, spiritual directors may be able to offer suggestions about helpful books, seminars or courses. For example, many people struggling with issues of faith have found the concept of Stages of Faith put forward by James Fowler[32] and others both illuminating and comforting.

In helping church leavers, those spiritual directors who are not clergy possibly have an advantage. People damaged by church are unlikely to seek out its professional employees for assistance, though for some it might feel safe to be with a director of a different denomination. At the same time a present or past EPC church connection in a spiritual director will be a qualifying factor for some people. Many EPC churches (like other kinds of church, and other social institutions) form subcultures of their own; subcultures with their own leaders, heroes, taboos, ethical standards, music, preferred writers and speakers, even their own dress code. People needing to process an exit from such a culture may find it easier to do so with someone who knows the jargon.

Some of the Christian subcultures are controlling and destructive. People who have formed their faith identity in such a culture may be deeply wounded in the process of leaving. The spiritual director may have to help them come to terms with hurt, anger, a sense of betrayal, guilt. There may also be loss and sadness as relationships are altered or destroyed.

How can a Spiritual Director help?

Part of the challenge of leaving church may be clarifying a sense of identity, answering the question 'who am I *now*?' Previously, identity may have been firmly anchored in a church community – but having rejected that, where can a new source of meaning be found? For some church leavers who come to spiritual direction, the issue may be to discover how their present story links up with their past. The spiritual director can be a listener who can help to make the connections, follow through the threads of continuity, and thus enable the church leaver to relish the present as the fruit of the past, with all its complexities. There is a danger in moving on: that present pain may poison the memory of what once was valuable and so prevent a person going with grace and freedom into something new. In telling their story at length and in depth, some people may discover that they don't need to wholly reject their past or the people they once were in order to become who God is now calling them to be.

This brings me to matters that may arise for spiritual directors accompanying church leavers and those who have issues with faith. Most are obvious and no different from those that occur in any spiritual direction relationship. If the director also has ongoing struggles with church, he or she will need to be wary of transference and parallel process potential. If the directee is at a different stage of faith, the director will need to be aware of that and respect it.

Most spiritual directors have reached the point in their faith journey where they are comfortable with mystery and paradox, have ample experience of many styles of prayer, and draw on many spiritual traditions for nourishment. It is sometimes possible to forget that people who come for spiritual direction don't share these assumptions, don't speak the same 'language', and may feel anxious and alienated by what their director takes for granted. The analogy of crossing cultures applies. People leaving church (whether literally or emotionally) and engaging with new ways of faith and prayer are entering a new culture and may experience the excitement and the apprehension of culture shock. The spiritual director needs to be able to help them through this transition.

How can a Spiritual Director help?

It is possible that some spiritual directors will experience pain to a greater or lesser degree as they accompany people engaged in rejecting church. Many of us may feel a strong impulse to bring in another perspective – to explain, to excuse, to defend. There may be occasions when another perspective is helpful and necessary. But people need to be heard first. One of the fundamental principles of Spirited Exchanges is that 'we let God defend God'. The institutional church has plenty of voices to defend it, and the person who feels wounded by church has certainly heard some of them. In the loving listening of a spiritual director such people may (consciously or unconsciously) sense an alternative embodiment of 'church'. That in itself provides a different perspective.

This study shows that very few people who have left church re-enter the same kind of church that they left. Of those who are described as Wayfinders, however, the majority do eventually connect with some sort of faith community – some describe it as 'church', others continue to reject that word. Thus spiritual direction has something further to offer church leavers – support and resources for those individuals who are making their way forward to a new wholeness of faith and a new engagement with a faith community.

13 A Pastor's Perspective

(Alan)

THE FIRST TIME I TENTATIVELY PRESENTED the findings of this study was to a small group of people in one of the options we offer as part of our Sunday morning services. It meant shifting hats continually from researcher to pastor and back again. The researcher in me was raising questions while the pastor side of me was being looked at for answers. Undeniably, this research provokes difficulties for churches – churches like the one I am part of. It was a threatening duality to try and hold. I found the researcher's role much easier. Raising the questions, pointing to the problems and illustrating the strength of the continued faith of leavers is one thing. Trying to deal with all the questions these stories of faith raise for the established church is quite another.

I am first and foremost a pastor. I started studying sociology because, as a pastor, I was concerned about understanding our culture so I could better communicate the gospel within it. I started studying why people leave the church because I was aware of peers who were leaving and because part of me was also leaving. When my thesis work was finished I returned to pastoral work and have stayed there.

So it is as a pastor that I want to reflect on the results of this study.

First I need to outline my understanding of what a pastor is. Biblically the image is drawn from the shepherd who cares for the flock. The Hebrew writers drew an analogy between the care of the flocks and herds and the care of God's people. In the scriptures God too is described as a shepherd. Significantly, Jesus also drew heavily on the image of a shepherd as leader of the people of faith.

Jesus talked about the distinction between good shepherds and hired hands. He called Peter to care for his sheep in the final chapter of John's gospel; and he praised the shepherd who would leave the 99 in search of the one who was lost.

In Ezekiel 34 God both castigates the idle shepherds and takes on the role of shepherd for himself.

> You have not strengthened the weak or healed the sick or bound up the injured. You have not brought back the strays or searched for the lost . . . . For this is what the sovereign Lord says: "I myself will search for my sheep and look after them. As a shepherd looks after his scattered flock when he's with them, so I will look after my sheep. I will rescue them from all the places where they were scattered on a day of clouds and darkness and I will bring them into their own land . . . I will tend them in good pasture, and the mountain heights of Israel will be their grazing land."

This understanding of the work of a pastor begins with the individual and with care for the individual. It claims that pastoral care – care for the whole person (spiritual, emotional, intellectual, physical, relational and missional) is the primary task of the pastor. This perspective informs preaching, the leading of worship, the decision processes of the local church, the corporate agendas of the local church and the hope of the local church for the future.

So it is with this understanding of what it means to be a pastor that I now consider these research findings. I want first to give attention to the place of the church.

A POST-CHURCH WORLD

The 'C' word is offensive to many today. Not only by those who leave the church but also many others who have never been part of it, the Church is seen as overwhelmingly boring, irrelevant, abusive and passé. A recent study in Australia on why people don't go to church put 'boring' at the top of the list. 42% of those asked said the reason they don't go is because it is boring and unfulfilling.[33]

It is hard to face up to, especially when your life's work is for the church. But we need to come to terms with the fact that Christendom is gone and the role of the church has moved from the centre of society to beyond the margins of significance for most people. It has moved to the point of being a dirty word. Until we face that reality we will not be ready to tackle the depth of the task ahead. This research reiterates the marginality of the church in two key ways:

1. The findings of this research indicate that having left, previously committed key leaders of EPC churches are very unlikely to return. Those that do will be in the minority. Most will continue to develop and strengthen their faith without participating in established churches.

2. There are increasing numbers of groups and personal supports for continued Christian faith beyond the church. The church leavers are forming and finding these resources. I believe that these groups can provide valuable insights from which we pastors in established churches can learn.

Taken together these two findings raise significant questions about the dominant approach to church leadership in many EPC churches in New Zealand today. Richter and Francis in *Gone but Not Forgotten* retell one of Jesus' parables[34] saying "which of you, having a hundred sheep, if you have lost one of them, does not say: 'we can't be bothered to look for strays. We've got a farm to run here! We can't risk the ninety-nine for the sake of just one. If the sheep has gone, it's gone. It's not our fault sheep are silly! We've got other important things to worry about[35]."

While the 'let's ignore the strays' philosophy reigns the church will continue to bleed and the centre of gravity of spirituality and faith will continue to move further and further away from church structures. It is increasingly my conviction, partly drawn from the results of this research and particularly respondents' views of church and church leadership, that the dominant push for structures and growth in EPC churches is a cry against the tide.

I believe, however, that there remains a huge role for churches and people who will take seriously the faith journeys of people, providing resources, support and companionship as they traverse the difficult places of faith and life.

I believe the church needs to learn how to listen: listen to people and listen to our culture. The greatest tool we have when working with church leavers is to listen. Listening helps them and it helps us as church leaders and pastors.

One of the most significant supports anyone can offer to people considering leaving a church or re-assessing their faith is to listen to them. Until they are heard they cannot hear! They need to be heard, really heard, before they are in a position where they can hear anything others might want to say. Therefore helping someone who is considering leaving or has left begins with a genuine commitment to try and understand their position and their feelings. We should not underestimate the power of such listening as a helpful, even healing, role in people's faith journeys. When such listening is non-judgemental and accepting it provides the context in which pains, abuses, questions, confusion, doubt and heartache can be verbalised and most importantly, heard. Something of the importance of this is summed up in a note from a respondent to the questionnaire:

> *Russell* Thanks for the opportunity to share these thoughts. I recently re-read the interview that you transcribed of my interview about five years ago. It is a valuable record for me. I had forgotten many of the issues and events that I described then . . . . This process is the only chance I have had since leaving the church to reflect and record my views for someone still in the church. It is a valuable and positive experience and I thank you for that.

People want to be heard but they want to be heard in particular ways. What are the qualities of such listening?

Non-judgemental Listening It is crucially important that the listening be non-judgemental. The majority of people struggling with church and faith have significant questions or hurts about church, the Bible, prayer and God and they need to talk about these. The listening they require is non-defensive. They need the kind of listening that does not try to defend the church or the Bible or even defend God. People need to be encouraged to verbalise what they feel and believe. If they are angry, let them talk about their anger. If they are hurt, let them describe that hurt and what it has done to them. If they have questions and doubts we let them put those 'out there' so they themselves and others also can see them objectively.

Face-value Listening Each person's story has to be taken at face value. At times people will make comments about church leaders or Bible passages or failed prayer that appear 'over the top', exaggerated, only half the story or simply untrue. At such times the kind of listening that is required is a listening that accepts that this is truth as it is experienced by this person right now. It is their truth, and whether or not others might agree it is the truth they are acting out of. It is true in its consequences.

Provisional Listening The corollary to face-value listening is provisional listening. Provisional listening means accepting that this is the person's viewpoint, feelings or understanding at this point in time. They may well change with time, and probably will.

Listening for the Unsaid Carefully watching body language and noticing emotions as well as arguments, pauses as well as words, is essential to the art of listening. Probing an emotion, pointing out a bodily reaction, naming a feeling can often open up new understanding and depths of communication.

Long-term Listening People's faith questions are not resolved quickly, their pain not healed instantly and their confusion does not clear in a night. Therefore the kind of listening that is required is long term. Realising this is both hugely daunting and positive for the listener. It is daunting because it reminds us that to really be a companion for this person then a substantial amount of time is required. It is reassuring because it reminds us that no matter how dark, angry or confused the person may be when we meet them and no matter how inadequate our responses may be, one conversation will never be 'the answer' but the long journey of many conversations.

Painful Listening The listener must really hear the pain of the other person. Their role is simply to absorb some of the person's pain – not minimising it, but sympathetically and if possible empathetically sharing in their pain and confusion. This is the kind of listening that hears the cry of the other person and takes on something of their pain and offers that pain in prayer to God.

Incarnational Listening As people raise their doubts, anxieties, past hurts and abuses, it is often helpful if they can be listened to by someone who represents, at least to some degree, the organisation, the faith, even the God whom they are questioning, railing against and attacking. This kind of listening is powerful. The following quote is taken from someone who has gone on a hugely difficult and grief-filled journey of faith:

> Even more valuable to me over this time was being able to talk with someone about all of it. Not just the big questions about God but also the horror and sense of abandonment that was the cause of it all. A person I trusted and came to highly respect, and who freely gave me time on a regular basis. This church figure gave me the freedom to say what I needed to say without judging and without trying to provide all the answers. Without suggesting I needed to return to church in order to find what I was looking for, this person provided options and caused me to think about things in new and different ways.

Notice the naming of this individual as a "church figure". The person's position as someone of faith and a 'church figure' added a quality to the listening. The fact that the person didn't suggest it was necessary to return to church is important; the fact that the one who said it was a 'church figure' increased significantly the power of the comment.

It is my growing conviction that 'post-church' groups need to include church leaders. While groups of like-minded church leavers outside of any church connection are undoubtedly helpful, they function in isolation from the church and the appointed leaders of the faith. It is one thing to be able to talk about my questions and doubts with a group of people who hold similar doubts, but it is quite another thing to be able to talk about these with someone who is part of the church. It is one thing to be able to talk about the way particular Christian scriptures have been used to abuse and disempower people with others who have similar experiences. It is another thing again to talk about these things with someone who teaches the scriptures in a church setting.

But I have a second reason for suggesting listening as the crucial tool for pastors. It is because I believe that as we listen, we change. Listening enables us to hear the perspective of those outside the church, both those who were once part of the church and equally those who have never been part of it. In this listening – non-judgemental, provisional, face-value, long-term, painful listening – we will hear the Spirit of God opening up new ways for us all.

Of course such listening by church leaders demands a lot. Firstly it demands that the leaders have walked their own dark nights of faith and have come to see the church in human history as a 'dysfunctional community of faith' which, like themselves, 'is now and ever will be' riddled with evil, incomplete truth and human agendas. And yet they also hold that this 'dysfunctional community' is a site of the Spirit's work, the bride of Christ and a community demanding their love and energy. It is the kind of listening that is willing to hold the tensions of all they believe the church should be and hope will be with the realities of their own and other people's experiences. Holding this tension means listening, listening without defensiveness, to someone's heartache about the church; their doubts about prayer or scripture; and their lack of belief in or disappointment with God. It means personally taking on the other person's hurt, anger and confusion while quietly and in an unspoken way connecting their feelings with the God who died for the church.

Such listening is a primary but neglected tool in the tool box, and it is the hope of the church of the future.

14 Postscript

IN THESE PAGES, AND IN OUR ENGAGING WITH PEOPLE who 'struggle with issues of church or faith or both',[36] we are dealing with several pairs of apparently polar opposites. We have wanted to respect individuality, and yet we've classified people into groups. We've entered into the pain and anger of people who reject the institutional church, yet we are ourselves committed to a local church in inner city Wellington. We aspire to be followers of Jesus, yet we are listening to the stories of people who are searching off the beaten track, or no longer describe themselves as Christian – as well as to the stories of those who are bravely re-defining what it means for them to have faith. To maintain integrity we must continue to feel the tension between these opposite poles.

THE INDIVIDUAL AND THE GROUPS

In the research we have been looking for common threads in order to generalise about what we presumed to describe as 'typical' of the categories we discerned among church leavers. At the same time we are extremely aware that each person is unique, that each journey is different, and that no one fits neatly into a box. We have talked of 'stages' of church leavers but it might be truer to talk of 'zones'. A zone is a space not defined by closed borders. For example, in the terms of this study, a person may be moving toward becoming an Explorer but still exhibit many of the traits of an Exile. Thankfully, there's no quick quiz to help you neatly classify another person – or yourself.

These categories can't be forced onto people, but we have become very certain of their usefulness. This was demonstrated at the first training weekend held for people interested in facilitating groups like Spirited Exchanges. Many of those who came had left church, others struggled at the fringe. They were introduced to the categories of the Displaced, the Exiles the Explorers and the Wayfinders not as a grid on which they might exactly plot their position but more as a pictorial map by which they might identify the zones through which they travelled.

Nearly all of the participants could track the pattern of their own journey on the 'map'; or could see how it would help them to understand another's story. As the group discussed what it might feel like to be in each zone and what images might symbolise that particular space there was clear agreement. People were not so much learning something new as recognising what they intuitively knew already.

So people nodded when they heard others describing how it feels to be Displaced: *isolated, powerless, angry, betrayed* and *misunderstood* were the adjectives used. In the discussion about the Exile space the group came up with some powerful images: "like being at a major intersection . . . like having a suitcase burst and scatter its contents all over the place . . . like looking at your own grave". Many of the group had experienced this stage and could identify with the feelings evoked by these pictures. By contrast, the sense of new life burgeoning, the beginnings of hopefulness and a restored energy to *do* not merely to talk: these were the elements that characterised the experience of those who described the Explorer zone. Once again, the majority of the group could recognise common ground.

Generalisations about a group can thus become a gift to the individual. Instead of locking a person into a stereotype, they can become a way of validating a person's story, and furthering self understanding.

BEING IN CHURCH – BEING WITH CHURCH LEAVERS

The second pair of polarities is more difficult. Alan and Jenny are both ministers at a Baptist church. Adrienne is involved as a deacon (member of the lay team of leaders) at the same church. There is at times a very strong tension between the two poles of commitment to church and commitment to church leavers. To accentuate the paradox, Spirited Exchanges, supporting church leavers, exists partly because it is sustained and supported by a local church. Yet most of its members would probably be disconcerted (at the very least) were they to attend a Spirited Exchanges meeting, just as many of those involved in such a group would find it very uncomfortable to re-enter a church service. It is not easy to be both loyal and honest in both genres. We possibly lay ourselves open to the charge of hypocrisy. To put it crudely: how can a minister, ordained to preach the gospel and teach the Scriptures, refrain from challenging, correcting and instructing people who have left church? Alternatively, how can a person sharing the doubts and struggles experienced by many church leavers confidently preach, teach and pray in a congregational setting?

The analogy of crossing cultures has been helpful here. It's not hypocritical, but respectful and humble to express ourselves differently according to the culture we are addressing. We can listen to another person's story without abandoning our own truth; and we can try to tell our own story in the language that our listeners understand.

The tension is undeniable and unavoidable, but it is usually more creative than destructive. Church leaders, if they so choose, have much to learn from church leavers. Their criticism may be hard to hear, yet if churches will listen to it they may be able to reform some of their destructive patterns and become safer, more honest and more compassionate.

A church building recently constructed in Wellington may provide a metaphor for a harmonising of the two genres. St Joseph's church has been designed as a cross enfolded by a koru.[37] Churches traditionally are built in cruciform shape and the architects wanted to retain yet reframe this. The koru, like a path, like a symbol of new life and growth, spirals around the central cross-space which is not walled off but open and accessible. The building is anchored in its city environment, taking

116

account of the lie of the land – like most of Wellington it's on the side of a hill. On a busy corner of two main thoroughfares it has a curving glass wall. Drivers and pedestrians can see in, people inside can see out. Visible, transparent, linked to the natural world, shaped by this particular city, incorporating Maori as well as Pakeha[38] symbolism, perhaps this building can symbolise a possible relationship between church lovers and church leavers.[39] Perhaps in this relationship there will be times when churches can hear the stories and draw from the life of those who have left; perhaps there can even be times when church leavers can acknowledge what has been good for them about aspects of church. Perhaps we can dream that a growing number of churches will become less concerned about who is in and who is out and more affirming of mature seekers who are 'working out their own salvation'.

BEING FAITHFUL – BEING DOUBTFUL

A third polarity is individual and personal. If we are committed to being followers of Jesus it can be disturbing, even painful, to listen to the stories of people who struggle with faith, or who reject it. Our own faith is frequently challenged and stretched – which is healthy, but also demanding. Another person's doubts can feed our own. We are not the wise persons who have settled every faith question, but just as much on the move as others who try to find their way forward to increasing wholeness.

It is our business to be honest. We owe it to ourselves as much as to the people we relate to. In maintaining personal integrity we're sustained by friendships in and outside of church. Spiritual direction and supervision help us to stay self-aware and be responsible for our own health. This tension in fact turns out to be healthy for us. Being engaged with those who struggle with faith requires us to nurture and scrutinise our own faith at all times. There is little chance of our falling into the trap of remaining Christian by default.

Churchgoing Christians, hearing about the work of Spirited Exchanges, sometimes want to use the words 'ministry' or 'mission'.

Postscript

These aren't words we're comfortable with, carrying as they do connotations of converting, reclaiming or rescuing those who have gone astray. It is a fundamental principle of Spirited Exchanges that there is no agenda to bring people back into the established church. Instead we seek to have an attitude that's not dogmatic but suggestive, not compelling but offering, not directive but tentative. If this is mission it's a different kind of mission: not trying to convince people of what to believe but to walk alongside them in order that they – and we – may stay on the track for truth. To trust the Spirit of God who "blows like the wind in a thousand paddocks inside and outside the fences".[40]

15 Methodology of the Study

(Alan)

As INDICATED IN THE FOREWORD, research of this kind is relatively rare. There has been little qualitative research in the area of church leavers,[41] and even less that specifically looks at the evangelical stream of the church. *A Churchless Faith* (2002) was a study of EPC church leavers in New Zealand. While it endeavoured to record people's complete faith journey up to the time of the interview there was no systematic follow up with interviewees. The study therefore recorded the faith perspective of each person at one particular point in time. Quite understandably this study was critiqued on two principal accounts:

1. The study was a slice in time. Although the study tried to track the journeys of 108 church leavers[42] from the point of joining an EPC church to the date of the interview there was no systematic ongoing tracking of interviewees within the study.[43]

2. The sample of 108 leavers was drawn from a snowballing[44] method and was therefore not a random sample or a significantly large sample. Some have suggested a truly random sample of 2000 or more respondents would provide a basis for verification of the findings.[45]

There were many reasons for using a snowballing method to find potential interviewees. Among them was the practical difficulty, using a purely random sampling technique, of locating people who had been committed to an EPC church as adults and had subsequently left. While this practical difficulty was considered to be quite substantial and certainly beyond the resources of one research student it was not, however, the primary reason for selecting a snowballing method. The primary reason related to the exploratory nature of the study. The research was opening up new ground, because there was no other significant research focused on the leaving of committed adult members of EPC churches. There was certainly none that sought to explore qualitatively the reasons for people's decision to leave and their subsequent faith journeys. The focus was, therefore, on developing potential explanations for why people leave and where they go. If, and at the time it was a big if, interviewees could be located and potential understandings drawn from their personal stories, these could then be subsequently 'tested' through later projects based on larger sample groups of randomly selected ex-EPC church attenders.

The first of these criticisms – that the study merely gave an understanding of the leaver's faith at one point in time – spurred this follow-up study. Five years after the last of the initial study interviews, the interviewees were sent questionnaires (see Appendix B) in order to determine how their faith journeys had changed over the subsequent years.

The original 108 interviewees were approached by mailing letters and questionnaires to their last known address to invite them to be part of the follow-up study. When there was no reply, or a returned envelope was received, follow-up addresses were searched through phone books and the internet and new letters sent. Letters were sent out on three occasions over a six month period to each address. 36 of the interviewees could not be located. Over the five to six years in question these people had moved and no forwarding address was able to be located. At the end of the six months of searching for people to take part in the study, 47 completed interview scripts were received. These 47 scripts represent 66% of the interviewees where an address was located, or 43.5% of the original 108 interviewees.

	N	%	% of interviewees located
Original number of interviewees		100%	
Died	1	0.92%	
Address not located	36	33%	
Returned questionnaires	47	43.5%	66%

A 66% return for a detailed questionnaire[46] requiring a substantial amount of each respondent's time and thought represents a very high return rate and provides a significant basis from which to draw conclusions. While a total number of 47 returns from a potential 108 interviewees may not look huge, the quantity and depth of information gained would lead me to argue that getting more questionnaires returned would not have changed the findings. In research terms, *saturation* had been reached. Researchers claim a saturation point has been reached when there would be no need to do further analysis of the data as it would only add 'bulk' to the data and nothing to the theory and would therefore be redundant to the analysis.

In the original study, interviewees were divided into five principal faith groupings. The table on the next page shows the number of returns and the respective percentage for each faith category.

	Total Number of interviewees Original Study	Returned questionnaires	%
Displaced Followers	19	6	31.5%
Reflective Exiles	32	11	34%
Transitional Explorers	19	7	37%
Transitioned to Alternative Faith	7	5	71%
Integrated Wayfinders	30	18	60%

FAITH CATEGORISATION FROM QUESTIONNAIRES

Each questionnaire was read by the three raters (Jenny McIntosh, John Sinclair and Alan Jamieson) independently and then categorised after discussion between the three raters. Each rater used the criteria developed in *A Churchless Faith* (see Appendix A). There was a very high degree of consistency in the ratings given.

ANALYSING INDIVIDUAL RESPONSES

The individual responses to each question were analysed by Adrienne Thompson and the responses compared for each category as well as between categories. Adrienne, a qualified Spiritual Director, brought her skilful listening to the questionnaire responses and helped to draw out some of the major themes that are discussed.

Whereas *A Churchless Faith* was the work of one thesis student, this follow-up study was worked on and the findings assessed by four people, all of whom have professional and personal experience in the area of study.

METHOD AND CATEGORISATION

In the original study the five faith categories were developed as the research progressed from the material gained through interviews.

Methodology

Characteristics of the different groupings of people were developed and these were subsequently used to ensure that each person, as described in their interview script, was appropriately assigned to one or other of the faith categories. Each of these categories is simply a diagnostic box which provides a best fit in each case. In the original study this work was done by myself.

The follow-up study allowed for the categories of the faith stages themselves to be assessed. In this case when the questionnaires were analysed they were considered on their own against the criteria for each faith category and on the basis of this analysis assigned to the different groups. In this particular study three people were involved in the analysis process, not just one. In this way the degree of subjectivity from one researcher was reduced.

APPENDIX 1

In order to assess where people could best be assigned among the different groups certain criteria were laid down. Individuals might not meet all the criteria for a particular category, but they did need to meet the majority of them in order to be included in that group.

Criteria for Displaced Followers

1. Left church because of specific church grumbles such as arguments, directional changes and leadership issues.

2. Left because of inappropriate or inadequate pastoral care at specific needy times in their lives. Thus they left feeling hurt, disappointed and disillusioned.

3. Retained unexamined, non-reflective faith. No sign of questioning fundamental assumptions. The basis of Scripture or creeds remains.

4. Hope that one day they will return to church.

5. Hope that God will start something new, a new style of church, way of operating etc that they can join.

6. Faith nurtured now by Christian radio stations, TV evangelists, seminars, Christian books, magazines, trans-denominational conferences and camps et cetera.

7. Faith practices (e.g.: 'Quiet Times', prayer, reading the Bible) continue; or if not, at least their value and importance is acknowledged.

8. Strong commitment to Christian faith.

Criteria used to Categorise Interviewees

Criteria for Reflective Exiles

1. A confused, unsettled and unsure state of faith. People make comments to the effect that they don't know or understand their faith anymore.

2. A claim that they are not denying their faith, but continue to believe. They are still Christians in their own eyes. Often this Christian faith is based on past events or experiences of God rather than present realities or experiences.

3. Leaving faith issues and practice. Putting their faith down and not addressing it at the moment.

4. Significant faith questions dominate their present faith.

5. A less condemning attitude to those who don't fit the 'in box' of evangelical Christianity; for example, greater acceptance of homosexuals.

6. Caution or wariness when it comes to considering reading the Bible or using it as a guide for faith and practice.

7. Strong negative feelings towards the church. These may include frustration, anger or sadness. A number of interviewees in this category will cry and become visibly upset during interviews as they talk about their time in the church.

8. Finding a new sense of self, of personhood and a new freedom within themselves to be who they are without reference to external expectations.

9. An aversion to Christian things, people or teaching.

Criteria for Transitional Explorers

1. Emerging self-owned and articulated faith – emerging confidence in Christian faith.

2. Personal responsibility taken for decisions. Seeing self as authority. Emergent sense of 'I'.

3. Taking responsibility for their faith, not willing to let it drift, know it is up to them to take some action to build, reflect on and develop their faith.

4. Re-establishing relationships with self-selected others and groups.

5. Desire for rational, bounded, comprehensive faith and world view understandings. Attempt to seek closure rather than allow tensions or paradoxes to remain open.

6. Desire for leadership structure that does not seek their dependency on it.

7. Respect for autonomy of others.

8. Focus on rational, thought-out, coherent faith

9. Prepared to include groups and others that have some ideological compatibility with the individual.

10. Symbols univocal and translated into explicit conceptual meanings.

Criteria for Integrated Wayfinders

1. A clear statement of Christian belief.

2. Have made decisions about aspects of God, Christ and Christianity. These are definite and settled and personal.

3. A sense of identity as a Christian. Their faith is an integrated part of who they are. This is part of the essence of their makeup.

4. A comfortable, settled nature to their faith (at rest). These are people who are relaxed and at ease with their faith. They are comfortable talking about their faith in a way that reflects the integrated nature of their faith and lifestyle.

5. These people have integrated their previous church experience into who they now are without obvious anger or frustration. There may be past disappointments or frustrations but these have been put behind them.

6. Associated with other like-minded Christian people, networks, faith groups or church commitment.

Criteria used to Categorise Interviewees

Criteria for Transition to Alternative Faith Position

1. Explicitly reject the word 'Christian' as a descriptor of their current faith and practice.

2. Have so many questions, doubts and issues with the Christian faith that they characterise themselves as 'agnostic' or 'atheist' in their belief system; *or*

3. Have chosen to describe themselves as 'new age' in outlook and practice.

APPENDIX 2

Five Years On Research Questionnaire

1. Do you consider yourself a person of faith today? If so, how would you describe your faith? What are the key components of it?

2. As you look back over the last five years are there any significant ways that your faith has changed from five years ago? If so, can you explain further? In responding to this question you may wish to comment on some or all of the following areas:

   a) Beliefs/Theology.
   b) Attitude towards other faith traditions or spiritual paths.
   c) View of prayer.
   d) What prayer is for you and what do you feel is happening when/if you pray.
   e) View of God. What are your thoughts or images of God (positive or negative) now?
   f) View of Jesus Christ and the Holy Spirit.
   g) The significance of the Bible.
   h) View of human nature and the purpose of human life.
   i) Do you have personally important faith/God experiences now?
   j) How you come to make moral and ethical choices.
   k) Faith as an impetus for our involvement in wider community action or service.

The Questionnaire

l) The notion of mission or sharing your faith.

m) Your image of a 'mature faith'.

n) View of the church.

3. Where do you feel that you are growing, changing or struggling with faith questions or doubt at this present time? Has this changed in any way over the last five years?

4. Are you presently involved in an established church? Or faith group? If so could you please describe the church or faith group and the ways you are involved and the reasons you choose to be involved in this group/church?

5. What do you regard as important components of leadership in a faith group or church?

6. Are there other supports to your faith that are significant for you now? E.g. Spiritual Direction, retreats, seminars, courses, books, magazines, TV or radio programmes.

7. Are there any religious rituals or symbols that are important to you now? Has their importance changed for you over the last five years?

8. Are there any significant changes in other areas of your life that may have impacted on your present faith position or view? E.g. living situation, family, educational, career or health.

APPENDIX 3

Swimming Beyond the Flags
by Alan Jamieson

Extract from an article called "Should I stay or should I go?"
first published in *Canvas* Magazine, Issue 4 1ˢᵗ Quarter 1997

IMAGINE GOING TO THE BEACH FOR THE FIRST TIME and finding that there are people swimming and playing in the water. These people offer to teach you to swim and enjoy the water. You become excited about the ocean and join them. For years you enjoy going to the beach regularly. Eventually you become a swimming instructor, teaching others how to swim between the flags, and you enjoy seeing them also become competent swimmers.

One day at the beach you wonder what it would be like to swim further, to go exploring the rock edges, or maybe to dive to the depths of the ocean. Over the weeks that follow, a yearning to go further begins to build within you. At the same time you become increasingly self-conscious about going swimming. It does not seem so much fun, or as much of a challenge as it used to be. You don't enjoy going to the beach like you used to, and maybe you become critical of all this swimming and playing.

Months later you find yourself almost resenting the beach. You tentatively mention to others your desire to go out deeper, to dive, to explore the pools and the depths. The coach gets to hear of your interest and warns you of the dangers of swimming outside the flags. He can tell stories of people who went out there and never came back. Instead he suggests you go to a swim-meet to rekindle your enthusiasm.

So you go to the swim-meet and that seems to help for a while. But then the vague yearnings return, stronger than before. You can't get out of bed to go swimming, and you find yourself making up all sorts of excuses. One morning you realise you have not been to the beach for three months or more. You wonder what to do next and after some days worrying about it you realise you don't ever want to go back again. All they do there is swim backwards and forwards and play in the waves. It was fun, even exciting for a number of years, and you thought swimming was all there was to life. But now 'it's just not where you're at anymore'. You remain a swimmer, after all no one can deny your experience of the ocean, but you choose to go to the mountains or somewhere else to do your exploring.

So another person leaves the sea of Christian faith, bored with what seems to be on offer near the beach and yet unaware of the many other options for exploring the ocean – scuba diving, snorkelling, deep sea diving . . . . Exploring these options does not mean losing or diluting your faith, but finding Christ in new ways. It can be a journey to greater personal conviction and commitment to Christ, and a more holistic and relevant faith.

This illustration is not designed to criticise churches that emphasise particular stages of the faith journey. We need churches that will focus on evangelism and train people to begin the journey with Christ. You can't go snorkelling or diving without being a proficient swimmer. What this does show is how some of our most committed people come to a point of needing to explore their Christian faith in other, perhaps radically different ways. To stem the flow of leavers we need to support them.

Canvas is published by
Tertiary Students Christian Fellowship,
PO Box 9672, Wellington

Bibliography

Below is a list of texts cited in this research or relating to it.

Barna, G (2005) *Revolution: Finding Vibrant Faith Beyond the Walls of the Sanctuary* Tyndale House Publishers; Wheaton.

Bellamy, J; Black, A; Castle, K et al. (2002) *Why People Don't Go to Church.* Openbook Publishers.

Davie, G (1990) *Believing without belonging: is this the future of religion in Britain?* Social Compass Vol 37, 455-469.

Davie, G (1994) *Religion in Britain Since 1945: Believing without Belonging* Oxford, Blackwell.

Dawn, M (1997) 'You have to change to stay the same' in Cray, G et al *The Post-evangelical Debate* London, Triangle. 35-56.

Drane, J (2000) *The McDonaldization of the Church: Spirituality, Creativity and the Future of the Church* London, Darton Longman Todd.

Fanstone, M J (1993) *The Sheep that Got Away: Why do People Leave the Church.* Tunbridge Wells, MARC.

Fowler, J W (1984) *Becoming Adult, Becoming Christian: Adult Development and Christian Faith.* San Francisco, Harper & Row.

Fowler, J W (1987) *Faith Development and Pastoral Care.* Philadelphia, Fortress Press.

Fowler, J W (1995) *Stages of Faith: The Psychology of Human Development and the Quest for Meaning.* San Francisco, Harper (first published 1981).

Fowler, J W (1996) *Faithful Change: The Personal and Public Challenges of Postmodern Life.* Nashville, Abingdon Press.

Fowler, J W & Keen, S (1985) *Life Maps: Conversations on the Journey of Faith* Berryman, J (ed) Waco, Texas, Word Books. (first published 1978).

Gilligan, C (1982) *In A Different Voice: Psychological Theory and Women's Development.* Cambridge Massachusetts, Harvard University Press.

Gilling, B (1992) Introduction, in Gilling B (Ed) *"Be Ye Separate": Fundamentalism and the New Zealand Experience.* Hamilton NZ, University of Waikato and Colcom Press. xi-xv.

Gilling, M (1999) *Where do We Find Our Meaning?* Auckland, Futures Group of the Methodist Church of New Zealand.

Grainger, R (1993) *Change to Life.* Darton Longman Todd.

Hagberg, J O & Guelich, R A 1989 *The Critical Journey: Stages in the Life of Faith.* Dallas, Word Publishing.

Hendricks, W D (1993) *Exit Interviews: Revealing Stories of Why People are Leaving the Church.* Chicago, Moody Press.

Hoge, D R, Johnson, B, Luidens, D A (1993) Determinants of church involvement of young adults who grew up in Presbyterian churches, *Journal for the Scientific Study of Religion*; Vol 32, No 3, 242-255.

Jamieson, A (2002) *A Churchless Faith: Faith Journeys Beyond the Churches.* London, SPCK.

Jamieson, A (2004) *Journeying in Faith: In and Beyond the Tough Places.* London, SPCK.

Johnson David & Van Vonderen Jeff (1991) *The Subtle Power of Spiritual Abuse.* Bethany House Publishers, Minnesota.

Lyon, D (2000) *Jesus in Disneyland: Religion in Post-modern Times.* Cambridge, Polity Press.

Mead, L B (1993) *The Once and Future Church: Reinventing the Congregation for a New Mission Frontier.* New York, Alban Institute Publication (first published 1991)

Parks, S (1986) *The Critical Years: The Young Adults Search for a Faith to Live By.* San Francisco, Harper & Row.

Peck, M S (1993) *Further Along The Road Less Travelled: The Unending Journey Toward Spiritual Growth.* New York, Simon & Schuster.

Pressau, J R (1977) *I'm Saved, You're Saved – Maybe.* Atlanta, John Knox Press.

Richter, P & Francis, L J (1998) *Gone but Not Forgotten: Church Leaving and Returning.* London, Darton Longman Todd.

Riddell, M (1998) *Threshold of the Future: Reforming the Church in the Post-Christian West.* London, SPCK.

Roof, W C (1993) *A Generation of Seekers: The Spiritual Journeys of the Baby Boom Generation.* San Francisco, Harper.

Stokes, K (1992) *Faith is a Verb: Dynamics of Adult Faith Development,* Mystic, Connecticut, Twenty-third Publications.

Streib, H (2002) *Varieties of Deconversion Experiences in the Federal Republic of Germany and the United States of America: Potentials for Transformation, Vulnerabilities, and Needs for Intervention.* An Exposé of Research project – unpublished research paper.

Tomlinson, D (1995) *The Post-Evangelical.* London, Triangle.

Ward, H and Wild, J (1995) *Guard the Chaos: Finding Meaning in Change.* London, Darton Longman Todd.

Footnotes

1 Barna, G *Revolution: Finding Vibrant Faith Beyond the Walls of the Sanctuary.* Tyndale House Publishers; Wheaton 2005

2 The questionnaire is reproduced as Appendix 2

3 *Backsliding* is a common term in evangelical circles to describe people whose faith is sliding backwards towards a loss of faith or unbelief.

4 *Specific grumbles* here contrast with the *meta-grumbles* articulated by the Reflective Exiles. The word *grumble* is used in a technical sense to describe issues that cause dissatisfaction and distress and does not imply that the issues are trivial.

5 Capital letters and underlining as cited, in this quotation and throughout this text.

6 'Quiet times' refer to a regular practice of bible reading and prayer, usually daily, often encouraged in evangelical church circles.

7 For a fuller discussion of the leaving process see *A Churchless Faith* (2002) SPCK pp 29-45.

8 For example: concerns about the leadership, church decisions and pastoral care which were the principal reasons the Displaced chose to leave.

9 See *A Churchless Faith* (2002) SPCK pp 85-89 for more details.

10 An umbrella term for spiritualities and beliefs based on a range of new and old eastern beliefs beyond orthodox Christian understandings.

11 More details of the criteria used to assign people to faith categories are supplied in Appendix 1.

12 Transcribing the first set of interviews was a formidable task. Each interview could take 8-10 hours. With a potential set of a hundred or more interviews this time (up to 1,000 hours) was simply not available.

13 In either their respective interviews in the original study or in the subsequent questionnaire responses.

14 After carefully analysing their original interview script and the subsequent questionnaires the conclusion was reached that they had been incorrectly categorised in the first study and should have been seen as Displaced from the beginning. In the original interview this couple didn't express any signs of anger at the church and did indicate positive signals of a stable faith beyond the church. It appeared that they didn't have the angst of the Exiles or Displaced and were therefore, incorrectly, seen as Wayfinders. How is this mis-categorisation possible? One explanation could relate to the way people can intellectualise a faith position beyond where they presently live out their faith and life. This implies that these people could intellectually describe and speak like Wayfinders while the actual living of their faith was best described as that of the Displaced. As these were highly intelligent, well educated, long term Christians this could be an explanation. Secondly and in a related sense, the Displaced and Wayfinders can appear quite similar in an interview setting. This is especially true

of well educated, theologically literate and articulate people who can give evidence of a breadth and depth of faith that appears to transcend the boundaries of an EPC package, but yet when really pushed finds its equilibrium in a typical EPC stance. Their questionnaire responses were clearly best described as those of Displaced Followers and a subsequent re-reading of their interview scripts, from five years ago, indicates that their position had not substantially changed. At times the faith of Displaced Followers and Integrated Wayfinders can easily be confused. Although they are a long way apart in terms of the journey covered, they often present in very similar ways and can express themselves similarly.

15 There may well be a large number of these disconnected (in terms of established church connections) Christian people. Certainly the Spirited Exchanges groups we run for church leavers, while not focused on the concerns of the Displaced, have had a reasonable number of people best characterised as Displaced turn up. A large proportion of them may be part of the fringe group at Christian gatherings sometimes identified as *spiritual butterflies*. The term is used to describe those who gently pass through seminars, special training events, worship meetings etc. but never stay long enough to become involved, connected or really known. One minister who has a keen interest in church leavers talked with me about advertising to reach this group of Displaced using the slogan *Love Jesus – can't stomach the church.*

16 Although these three continue to be involved in an established church it is not an EPC-style church either in theology or practice. And their participation is limited.

17 The complete questionnaire is given in Appendix 2.

18 In my judgement [Adrienne wrote after analysing these responses to the questionnaire], only one person appears to have moved to the far edge or possibly outside of an orthodox historical Christian faith. However the language they use is different from conservative EPC faith.

19 One Displaced Follower said 'not really' in answer to the question.

20 One mentioned that TV or radio programmes can be helpful on rare occasions.

21 *Reality* (which discontinued publication in June 2005) and *Stimulus* are New Zealand Christian periodicals.

22 A few guidelines that are stated at the beginning of a Spirited Exchanges discussion to ensure that it is a safe place for all who come. A complete list is given in Chapter 10.

23 "Weighing up the heart" from *My Heart Goes Swimming: New Zealand Love Poems* edited by Jenny Bornholdt and Gregory O'Brien. A Godwit book published by Random House, NZ 1996.

24 *Canvas* Magazine is published four times a year by the Tertiary Christian Students Fellowship of New Zealand (TSCF), PO Box 9672 Marion Square, Wellington. An extract from the article appears as Appendix 3.

25 Wellington Central Baptist Church has hosted and in numerous ways provided for Spirited Exchanges since it began, and along with the Dove Trust has supported it financially. Without its backing and risk taking it would not have been possible.

26 M Scott Peck. *The Different Drum*, Arrow Books Ltd., London, 1990. p 68.

27 from *The Subtle Power of Spiritual Abuse* by David Johnson & Jeff Van Vonderen. Bethany House Publishers, 1991, Minneapolis, Minnesota. pp 20, 21.

28 *A Churchless Faith* (2002) SPCK p 99.

29 Re-evaluation at this time of life is a universal life stage landmark and not infrequently results in re-expression of one's earlier faith paradigms. Gerald O'Collins speaks of it as a second journey which takes us to new and unexplored terrain. Mary D'Apice in her book *Noon to Nightfall* describes it as a time when the whole context of faith or philosophy of life is re-examined – what has been received from parents and other significant authority figures must now become our own. She also says that for the most part God seems strangely absent in this process.

30 Some of the material in this chapter is taken from my research paper *Spiritual Direction through Faith Stage and Cross Cultural Transitions* submitted as part of my training with Spiritual Growth Ministries Formation Programme and available on the SGM website: www.sgm.org.nz/research_papers.htm

31 *A Churchless Faith* (2002) p 130 and *Journeying in Faith* (2004) p 6

32 Fowler, James W *Stages of Faith: The Psychology of Human Development and the Quest for Meaning* 1985. HarperCollins Paperback Edition 1995

33 Bellamy, J; Black, A; Castle, K et al *Why People Don't Go to Church.* Openbook Publishers, 2002

34 Luke 15:4-7

35 See Richter, P & Francis, L J (1998) *Gone but Not Forgotten: Church Leaving and Returning.* London, Darton Longman Todd.

36 from the Spirited Exchanges website: www.spiritedexchanges.org.nz

37 *koru* is the Maori word for the spiral-curved fern fronds of New Zealand's native bush; and is also a classic motif in Maori art

38 *Pakeha:* European New Zealander

39 A detailed description of the church can be found at:
http://www.city-gallery.org.nz/mainsite/st-joseph-s-hato-hohepa1.html

40 James K Baxter "Song to the Holy Spirit" from *Collected Poems*, edited by J E Weir, Oxford University Press, New Zealand Branch, 1979

41 The most extensive study being that of Richter P and Francis L (1998) *Gone But Not Forgotten; Church Leaving and Returning.*

42 Including a small group (ten people) who had not left their particular church but were considering leaving and felt alienated within their church communities and environments.

43 A small number of interviewees were, however, informally tracked in that I met with them more than once throughout the course of the research.

44 A snowballing technique was employed in order to find interview respondents. At the time of starting the research I knew of a small number of potential interviewees whose names had been given to me by people on the margins of EPC churches. The snowballing technique then led to more and more church leavers from this particular stream of the church. After completing the initial set of 25 interviews I reviewed what common characteristics (of leavers) the snowballing technique was producing. This review revealed that the sample was potentially skewed. The interviewees referred to me were predominantly leavers from EPC churches. The snowballing technique was not leading to people who had left Quaker churches, Catholic churches or non-charismatic Protestant churches.

45 A larger international study comparing church leavers and those who stay as members of particular churches is presently underway in four regions of Europe and the United States (See Streib – 'Exposé of Research Project' in the bibliography for further details.)

46 The questionnaire is demanding in two respects. Firstly it involves four A4 pages of open questions. This necessitates a large amount of thought and time to answer. Secondly the questions probe personal issues about faith and the individual's personal life. Because of the length, the open nature of the questions and the personal nature of the material the return rate was very positive.